THE
CONNECTED LEADER

THE
CONNECTED
LEADER

Creating agile organizations
for people, performance and profit

Emmanuel Gobillot

KoganPage

LONDON PHILADELPHIA NEW DELHI

First published in Great Britain and the United States in 2007 by Kogan Page Limited.

First published in paperback in 2008
Reprinted in 2008, 2012, 2013

120 Pentonville Road	1518 Walnut Street,	4737 / 23 Ansari Road
London N1 9JN	Suite 1100	Daryaganj
United Kingdom	Philadelphia PA 19102	New Delhi 110002
www.koganpage.com	USA	India

© Emmanuel Gobillot, 2008

ISBN 978 0 7494 5276 6

British Library Cataloguing-in-Publication Data

A CIP record for this book is available from the British Library.

Library of Congress Cataloging-in-Publication Data

Gobillot, Emmanuel.
    The connected leader : creating agile organizations for people, performance and profit / Emmanuel Gobillot. — 1st ed.
        p. cm.
    ISBN 978-0-7494-5276-6
    1. Leadership. 2. Leadership—Case studies. 3. Organizational change. 4. Organizational change—Case studies. I. Title.
    HM1261.G63 2008
    303.3 4—dc22

                                                                2008005024

Typeset by Datamatics Technologies Ltd., Chennai, India
Printed and bound in Great Britain by 4edge Ltd, Hockley, Essex.

To Charlotte and George

Contents

Acknowledgements

It would be strange for a book that outlines the value of co-creation to have been written without the help of others. Many people have contributed to this volume in many ways. Indeed the ideas in this book are the results of happy occurrences and chance encounters that have influenced my view of the world. Whilst it is impossible to thank all the people who knowingly or unknowingly have shaped who I am, there are some individuals whose direct contribution to this book made it possible.

First, I have to go back, way before I had any thoughts on leadership to a time when I could not even understand the word. I want to thank Melvyn Elphee who, in my formative years at the United World College of the Atlantic, took a young Frenchman who had just arrived in Wales and taught him how to speak and write in English. In no way is he responsible for my less-than-sophisticated turn of phrase but I owe him the ability to avoid split infinitives. I can assure him that, after 20 years of living in England, this Frenchman no longer confuses 'tights' and 'thighs'!

Once I had set my mind on writing about a new kind of leadership and spoken often about the idea of connections, it was the encouragement and kind words of Professor Richard E Boyatzis (author and co-author of some of the most seminal works in the field of leadership), exchanged as we shared speaking platforms, that gave me the impetus to start typing.

The Hay Group UK management team offered me the chance to make this project a reality by giving me time and resources, first under the stewardship of Nick Boulter and latterly with the support of Graham Martin. A member of the management team who has supported me throughout this adventure is my divisional director, Chris Bowers, who has been a personal and professional source of strength. I also would like to convey my apologies to Chris Shennan and Dilum Jirasinghe, managers of the consumer and retail sector teams, who have shown great patience with me, as I did not support them or their teams as much as I would have without the distraction of writing.

Many of you will know, however, that little in an organization happens with the help of the management teams and senior colleagues alone. I want to thank two people who have protected me from myself whilst trying to consult and write at the same time. Hedieh Mirjafari kept me on the straight and narrow by making allowances and extending deadlines as I struggled to file financial returns and expenses claims on time. Pamela McGuire, my assistant, managed to work her way through my publisher's formatting requirements without suffering the breakdown these would have induced in me.

A number of colleagues have been kind enough to offer their thoughts and advice in a way that a sensitive author struggling to express his ideas could cope with. In particular I owe a lot to Graeme Yell for being the first person to read the early drafts and influence the shape of this book. My thanks also go to Stephen Cunningham, who pushed my own thinking forward by challenging the ideas contained in this book. Both are not only fine colleagues and valued friends but leading practitioners in the field of leadership and organizational change. It has been and remains a privilege to work with them.

I also want to thank my colleagues from the Hay Group McClelland Center for Research and Innovation in Boston, United States, for their time and support in helping shape this book. Mary Fontaine, Director of the Centre, and Signe Spencer were generous with both their time and their insights and as a result helped shape this book. Jim Burruss was kind enough to share his views on leadership and introduce me to the work of anthropologist Colin Turnbull, which had on me the great impact I suspect he has had on most who have come across his work.

This book could also not have been written without the help of Hay Group Education under the leadership of Russell Hobby. Russell and his team are tireless researchers and innovators in the field of leadership and many of the ideas and concepts you are about to encounter have come from their work. I owe them a great deal not only as a professional but also because their work fills me with the passion necessary to continue to want to learn about and push the boundaries of our understanding of leadership.

My thanks also go to the many clients who have influenced this book. In particular, thank you to Simon Machin, Head of Development, and Dave Ormesher, People Development Director at BELRON, Karel Foltyn, Human Resources Director at Unilever in the Czech Republic, Phillippa Hird, Human Resources Director, and Frances Merrylees, Head of Leadership Development at ITV, for trusting me enough to let me loose on their organizations.

Thank you also to all the people who have contributed case material. There are three leaders in particular who have managed to set aside their humility long enough to allow me to tell their story without having to resort to anonymity: Gary Lubner, Dave Neil and Simon Fell. Thank you to the three of them for their help and for giving this project time in their busy schedules.

I also wish to thank my publishers, Helen Kogan, Viki Williams, and their team at Kogan Page in the UK and the United States for giving a new author the chance to be heard and for supporting me during the publishing process.

Most importantly, you would not be holding this book if it hadn't been for the support, coaching and mentoring of a special and patient colleague. Helen Murlis, herself the author of many books and co-author of *Reward Management* (the bible of all things reward), has had to cope with strange calls and anxious e-mails as I lost my way and courage many times during this project. It has been a privilege to explore these unfamiliar territories with such a fine guide by my side.

To all of them I owe the fact that I have survived two very challenging years. However, the usual disclaimer applies: please blame me for any shortcomings and thank them that there are not more.

Introduction

If good leadership is about getting your staff to follow then, surely, great leadership has to be about getting your customers to do the same. But here is the problem: the very actions that ensure good leadership are the ones that will stop you from being a great leader. Welcome to the ultimate leadership paradox.

GOOD LEADERS ALWAYS EVENTUALLY FAIL

As night fell on Downing Street, London on 26 July 1945, it must have been hard for Winston Churchill to believe that the British people he had led to victory in the Second World War had so unanimously rejected him as a leader. Despite opinion polls showing his opponent in the lead from the start, no one (including the Soviet leader, Stalin) believed that Churchill would lose his job as prime minister. Clement Attlee, the man who was to replace him, could not believe he had won the election either. He had. The British people had spoken. Churchill the leader of the Conservative Party wasn't as appealing as Churchill the war hero. His campaign posters said 'Let him finish the job.' The British people didn't let him.

The problem with situations

But Churchill wasn't the only wartime leader rejected by peacetime electors. General de Gaulle also faced the wrath of the electorate. Being rejected by people you have fought for is not the preserve of European leaders. The youngest-ever superintendent of West Point and a key architect of Japanese democracy as Supreme Commander of the Allied Power in Japan, General MacArthur too was rejected by electors in his bid to become tenant at the White House in 1952.

Most leaders know that leadership is situational. It is about using the right style, with the right person, in the right situation. Could Churchill, de Gaulle and MacArthur be examples of leaders who didn't adapt to, or who misread, a new situation?

You only have to take a cursory glance at the speeches of these men to realize that this cannot be the explanation. All three had an incredible capacity for adapting their message to the situation at hand. From Churchill's 'We will fight them on the beaches' to de Gaulle's 'France has lost battles but has not lost the war' via MacArthur's Terminator-like pronouncement 'I shall return', all three knew what was needed and when. Their distinguished careers speak for themselves. It is impossible to win a conflict on the scale of the Second World War without engaging each and every one of your generals in the fast-moving theatre of battle. Churchill, de Gaulle and MacArthur were not only good situational leaders; they were masterful in their reading of situations. So why were they rejected? Where did they go wrong?

The power of context

What all three failed to respond to was not so much a change in situation as a much more fundamental change – a change in context.

That fateful 1945 election was the first in Britain for 10 years. During the war, Britain was changing. A new consensus was developing that called for new measures. In December 1942, social reformer Lord Beveridge published a report laying out radical responses to this radical change (a new welfare state and a national health service). This received only a lukewarm response from Churchill, who was busy adapting to the situations of war. In the words of Margaret Thatcher, 'Conservatives, with Churchill in the lead, were so preoccupied with the urgent imperatives of war that much domestic policy, and in particular the drawing-up of the agenda for peace, fell largely to the socialists in the Coalition Government.'[1] On the eve of the elections, having undergone the horror and deprivation of war, the British electorate wanted something different.

Focused on responding to situations, Churchill, de Gaulle and MacArthur failed to sense the broader change.

The leadership paradox

Leadership is a strange paradox. In order to be successful, leaders must adapt to the situations they face. Yet, by focusing on these situations, they often miss the radical shifts that are occurring around them. In effect, whilst trying to spot and adapt to changing events, leaders run the risk of missing a change in era. In an effort to address short-term challenges, they are forced to become short-sighted.

Good leaders always develop customer insights in the same way. They read the situation, bring back their understanding internally, conduct some analyses to establish the best response and deploy a solution through their structural teams (eg functions, geographies). This not only takes time but makes every situation appear more linear than it truly is. Good leaders are good at engaging staff, so they willingly follow, but that's no longer enough. To be agile enough to respond to context change, the whole organization, not just its leaders, needs to be attuned to stakeholders' changing expectations.

As internal and external complexity grows, structural teams no longer have either all the answers or the solutions. To sense a change in context and have the agility to respond, leaders must rely on people outside the boundaries of their functions, geographies and organizations. Their 'intact' team must give way to 'impact' teams. Great leaders get customers to follow them by creating communities and connections that sense changes and co-create responses to them.

THE PEOPLE ECONOMY

Fast-forward 60 years from the Second World War and once again a change in context is taking place. Like the context changes before it, this one is easily missed by leaders focusing on situations. Churchill missed the Beveridge report, de Gaulle misjudged social unrest and MacArthur failed to sense the advance of communism in Korea, but missing the signs doesn't mean they are not there. It is ironic that, over the last 50 years, the consumption economy has contributed to customers' emancipation and that it is that very emancipation that is now threatening the organizations that created it. The signs are plain to see.

Birth of a new context

Economic drivers change. The consumption economy had an elegant simplicity. You built something. They wanted it. They bought it. Over time, oversupply made things more difficult and brands (in one form or another) were established as the key differentiators. The idea was simple. You still built the product, but now you branded it. They wanted it because it had your brand on it. They bought it. But a brand that isn't lived is an empty slogan. Tired of deaf and mute brands, customers demanded more. The experience economy was born. Here is how it works. You build a product, but now you create an experience to go with it. They want it because the experience makes them want to belong. They buy it. This is not dissimilar to the consumption economy, but simple ideas find it hard to go away! But slowly, almost as surreptitiously as changes in the mood of the war generation, customers have learnt to like the experience so much that they no longer want it to be yours. They want to be in charge.

My life – my experience

A new breed of customers is being born, one that is changing the very foundation of how business is done. We are witnessing the arrival of a new economy, not technology driven this time but meaning driven. No longer are customers looking for an experience or employees wanting a salary. Human beings now long for meaning.

This has profound implications for the way we as human beings approach consumerism and consumption. Leaders beware: the new Beveridge report is being written.

The people economy is an economy where people rather than organizations are in charge. It is now futile for the organization to build a product betting on a customer wanting to buy it. The people economy requires organizations to co-create with customers. This they can only do if they transform themselves into communities that are of value to the self-actualizing customer. For this to happen, leadership must change.

THE CONNECTED LEADERSHIP CONCEPT

To ensure that their organizations are resilient to context change, leaders must make them agile. Agility requires all members of an organization to be fully engaged in order to respond to the changes they sense (whether or not these fall within their remit). Even if they have such insight, stakeholders are frequently faced with a 'formal' organization that stifles their opportunity to do anything about this. Designed with structures and processes aimed at task completion, the 'formal' organization is always slow to respond to unplanned context change.

There is however another way to look at an organization. The 'real' organization is made up of the networks of relationships people have within (and outside) the 'formal' organization. This is the organization leaders can rely on for agility. As a network, this 'real' organization is robust and flexible. To be a great leader is not to be able to lead the 'formal' organization but rather to channel the vitality of the 'real' organization towards the delivery of the 'formal' organization's objectives. It is this ability that I call 'connected leadership'.

A six-point journey

In this book I set out to demonstrate the following leadership proposition:

1. No longer do customers respond to products and services sold on economic incentives but rather, if they are to engage fully with and remain loyal to the organization, they seek reciprocity through moral and social obligations. The people economy is characterized by the need of customers to engage with communities that enable them to co-create meaning.

2. Organizations built on formal accountabilities not only find it hard to cope with reciprocity but they actively destroy it. This is what creates a disconnection between organization and people. Unaddressed, this disconnect will only grow as the people economy strengthens.

3. Leaders influence the engagement of people in two ways: traditionally, through the formal authority conferred upon them by their position, and, as well as this, through the informal authority rooted in their personal credibility. It is this informal authority that is critical to the success of leaders who are faced with responding to a new context (the people economy).

4. To succeed, connected leaders use their personal influence to recon-
   struct the social networks inside their organizations. These webs of
   informal connections (the 'real' organization) are critical to effective
   organizations because they lubricate the formal structure, spread
   expertise and innovation and create the flexibility needed to respond to
   the demands of the people economy. They effectively ensure that customers fully engage with the organization.

5. Connected leaders have developed three key components of connected
   leadership that create social and moral connections:
   - They are trustworthy and have trust in others. This enables the
     organization to manage the risks of co-creation with the customer.
   - They give meaning to relationships by uniting stakeholders around
     a shared agenda.
   - They encourage dialogue and powerful conversations as a way to
     secure engagement.

6. By understanding the characteristics of connected leaders and develop-
   ing them, two valuable goals are achieved:
   - The 'real' organization is developed and cultivated, either by
     increasing the web of connections and deriving general benefits, or
     by realigning connections to match the formal organization. Both
     approaches build sufficient agility to ensure customer engagement
     and resilience to context change.
   - Leaders facing increasing role ambiguity perform more effectively
     to benefit their organization and themselves.

FOUR PARTS, SEVEN CHAPTERS AND FIVE STEPS

Like you, I read business and leadership books. Probably like you, I am
taken in by bold claims and disappointed once they turn out to be nothing more than 'common sense'. Most insights are common sense, mainly
because, by the time we have heard them, they make so much sense that
we think we have known them to be true all along!

In my experience, though, in organizations today common sense is not
actually all that common. Many common-sense ideas contained in
management books are seldom implemented. Therefore, my aim with this
book is to translate the above proposition into something that you will see

the value of and know how to implement. To do so, I have structured the book in four parts.

Part 1: The case for connections

Part 1 builds the case for a new form of leadership. It explores why connections are the only way to make a business agile through being able to respond constantly to customers' changing needs. It also shows how organizations can adapt to this challenge.

Chapter 1 explains the limits of our traditional thinking about how people get engaged by organizations. It sets out the conditions for successful engagement of individuals beyond what they *have* to do to what they *want* to do. This will show you why current leadership tactics are limited to the current context and why your organization needs to be able to adapt to a new context that I will call the people economy.

Chapter 2 shows how organizations in their current form cannot meet the needs of people economy stakeholders. It explains how to capitalize on social networks to reconnect the expectations of stakeholders to the organizational performance needs. It highlights the key elements leaders need to address to build powerful webs of relationships between their customers and the organization.

Part 2: The case for connected leadership

Part 2 looks more closely at the kind of leadership needed to respond to the needs of the people economy.

Chapter 3 defines the role of leader in the people economy. It shows how a leader's impact is the new currency of engagement. It describes the key areas people focus on when deciding whether they will engage with a leader or not.

Chapter 4 describes the drivers of a leader's impact. It shows how a leader's impact comes from that leader's beliefs about what is desirable or not. It shows how these beliefs (which made leaders successful in the past) are now stopping leaders from becoming resilient to the new context. It offers a set of beliefs that underpins success in the people economy.

Part 3: The levers of connected leadership

Part 3 details the key components of connected leadership and what connected leaders do to capitalize on each of these.

Chapters 5, 6 and 7 take in turn each of the three critical building blocks of connected leadership impact (trust, meaning and dialogue). They show you what connected leaders are doing to create engagement. These are the tactics that will help you build new connections and ensure your resilience within the people economy by changing the nature of your impact.

Part 4: Developing connected leadership

Finally, Part 4 describes the development journey necessary to achieve connected status. Together, these five steps describe the components of the journey that will help you ensure your organization is fully connected to its stakeholders and therefore resilient to the change of era:

▌ Step 1: Understand the 'real';

▌ Step 2: Map out the 'formal'/'real' gap;

▌ Step 3: Evaluate your impact;

▌ Step 4: Develop connected leadership characteristics;

▌ Step 5: Build a supporting context.

What connected leadership doesn't say

It would be wrong to say that everything in this book is new and even more disingenuous to say that this book replaces everything that has gone before it. The success of connected leaders rests on their ability to understand what to change and what to keep. It is worth highlighting therefore that there are three key things this book does *not* say:

▌ *Traditional, hierarchical and technical management is obsolete.* This matters as much as ever and, the more leadership becomes a shared responsibility in complex organizations, the more important clarity and accountability become. However, a leader's relentless focus on the effectiveness of the organization's 'formal' instruments only leads to disconnections between the business and its customers. To be truly effective, an organization requires healthy informal connections that ensure agility, as well as clear vertical accountabilities that foster a culture of execution.

▌ *It is all about the individual leader.* In this book, I will focus on the individual leader in the organization context. The downfall of most leadership development over the last 20 years has been to overemphasize leaders' personal impact on organizational performance. For leaders seeking to get on ever-increasing executive pay scales this emphasis is good news, but for the majority sacked after only four years in post it shows how little one person alone can do. A single leadership focus might suffice inside the 'formal' organization, but connected leadership requires us to understand the intricacies of a leader's impact on the organization's system. To succeed, we need to bring together leadership and organizational effectiveness.

▌ *Connected leadership is new.* In many ways it is as old as organizations themselves and probably older; perhaps though it is coming into a greater focus as we seek to create organizations that are more flexible and responsive. It is certainly more relevant than ever given customers' renewed focus on connections and trust as drivers of sustainable long-term profitable relationships. Connected leadership is not a novelty.

ONE LAST THING

I understand that most of you are busy. Many of you will adopt varying approaches to taking away the messages this book contains. To make this volume an approachable read and cater for your varying needs, I have tried to prepare for every eventuality.

Questions this chapter will answer

At the beginning of each chapter, I set out the questions I seek to answer. If, having read the connected leadership proposition above, you have specific questions you would like answered, this is where you might want to start. There is no need to be sequential to be connected!

The 30-second recap

This book can be read in about five minutes, since each chapter finishes with a 30-second summary. If you are the skimming type, feel free to go straight to these. Reading these alone however will require you to take quite a bit 'on trust'. If you don't (and, after all, why should you?) then you may need to read the chapter!

The leadership takeaway box

At the end of each chapter, I have summarized the key messages for leaders (ie what this chapter means for the way you lead). If you are interested solely in what you should do (the 'so what'), without needing the why, this is the box for you. I have highlighted the 10 critical lessons learnt by connected leaders. The takeaway box will give you details of each of them:

1. Motivation exists in everyone – it is your job to find it.

2. Your organization is a community of individuals looking to co-create, not a collection of human resources waiting to deliver.

3. Bribery is no longer a performance management option.

4. Focus on relationships not structures.

5. Leadership is about being followed.

6. Your impact as a leader dictates organizational outcomes.

7. Power is the great motivator.

8. Manage your trust account.

9. Switch on your clarity positioning system.

10. Create dialogues.

Diagnostic tools

Parts 1, 2 and 3 end with a series of questions and exercises designed to help you test each of the concepts introduced in that part against your own situation. If you are ever in doubt that what has been described in the chapters you have just read applies to you or your business, you may want to use these questions as a focus for reflection.

Part One

The case for connections

- In 2000, worldwide consumption expenditures topped $20 trillion, a fourfold increase over 1960.[1]

- As of 2003 there were more private cars in the United States than licensed drivers.[2]

- Fifty-one of the 100 largest economies in the world today are corporations.[3]

- Despite these unprecedented rates of consumption, disconnects between people and business are emerging as never before.

In June 2003 something incredible happened in the United States. In the three days following the opening of the 'do not call' registry, 13.6 million people barred telemarketers from calling them. That's around 158 phone numbers added to the list per second. By March 2004, 58 million numbers were on the list. The mobilization of around 50 million people in the United States (assuming that some people will have more than one number) against one of the most representative business practices of the late 20th century has to be a worrying sign for any business leader.

Nevertheless, versed in the art of good leadership, leaders are adopting coping strategies. They plead with customers – explaining the need for telemarketing. They spin the message – describing telemarketing as an information service. They make legal challenges – successfully appealing to the courts to allow the use of pre-recorded messages.[4] Telemarketing is fighting for its status as the last legal form of stalking. Like Churchill reading an extract from the Beveridge report, leaders are mistaking the need to respond to a fundamental change in context for a situation needing a solution.

In the following two chapters, I want to introduce you to Samantha and Michael (a couple of singles looking for love on the internet), Maria (a successful jazz orchestra conductor), Torsten (a less-than-archetypal golfer) and Charlotte (my unruly eight-year-old daughter). The five of them will show you how to lead to ensure that your customers follow. The way they behave carries important lessons for the way in which you understand and build your organization.

1

What do people want?

Samantha H is 26. She is English, blonde, has a 'gsoh' (good sense of humour) and does not smoke. Michael S is 35. An American with a 'receding but cool haircut', he too is a non-smoker with a 'gsoh'. We can only hope for their own sakes that the apparently well-suited Samantha and Michael discover each other. Even if they don't, though, they will nevertheless be spoilt for choice.

Experiencing unprecedented rates of growth, online dating is set to become a $650 million industry by 2008. As an estimated 73 per cent of US singles use the internet to look for a partner, Michael has cause for optimism. With two out of three daters finding a partner online, he should not be single for much longer. As one in five singles in the UK uses the net to find a soulmate, Samantha too is likely to realize her dream. With dating industry conversion rates averaging 25 per cent, she should do well.

I do not know Samantha or Michael personally so their motivation is anyone's guess. But what I know about them is that, by their actions, they are standard-bearers of an unavoidable change in the way you work and build your organization. Through their behaviour, both are creating the biggest upset to the way you lead.

The questions this chapter will answer

▌ What drives engagement (no dating pun intended) and why does it matter?

▌ How is the nature of engagement changing?

▌ What are the new rules of engagement?

WHAT DRIVES ENGAGEMENT AND WHY DOES IT MATTER?

By looking for partners online, Samantha and Michael are not just using technology to build relationships; they are helping to shape a new trend.

The way we invest our energy and relate to each other is changing. This has profound consequences for the way leaders and organizations engage individuals. The Samanthas and Michaels of this world are standard-bearers of the new rules of customer engagement:

▌ They want to be engaged in something bigger than themselves yet they are distrustful of organizations.

▌ They are looking for meaning in their lives yet they reject organization-dictated experiences.

▌ They are becoming ever more focused on themselves as individuals yet they yearn to be members of communities.

▌ They want to be secure in deep relationships yet they do not want to be dependent.

The rules of engagement

How do you engage customers when, given so many paradoxes, every single one of your actions is likely to have unintended consequences?

The good news is that psychologists tell us that, as human beings, we have a constant need to engage. Professor and former chairman of the

Department of Psychology at the University of Chicago Mihaly Csikszentmihalyi describes an engaged individual as being 'in flow'. 'People in flow are exhilarated and are remarkably unstressed even when doing challenging work. They lose themselves in a task they love and feel "out of time". Their brains work efficiently and precisely.'[1] Working on exciting projects, completing a life-affirming task or simply shopping has led many to that 'out of time' state where people are fully invested.

So what are the conditions that will ensure the release of engagement? As Csikszentmihalyi observes, 'flow occurs most often when tasks are tightly aligned with a person's goals'. Leaders must find a way to understand the goal of human beings. Enter Samantha and Michael.

The search for meaning

The goal of Samantha and Michael, like that of any other human beings, is to self-actualize – to search for their true identity.

The concept of self-actualization is not new. Most of us have learnt about Maslow's hierarchy of needs. The hierarchy of needs is a great way to segment the world. We don't even think about it any more; it's just part of our shorthand for understanding people. Abraham Maslow published his theory in 1943.[2] Despite the well-documented lack of evidence to support his work, his is one of the most popular and frequently cited theories of human motivation. He divided human needs into two categories: deficiency needs and growth needs. The idea is that, until you have satisfied your deficiency needs, you will not begin to focus on your growth needs.

The first concern or the last resort?

However, whilst starting from a valuable insight, most leaders end up with a failed engagement strategy. They assert that only people with high levels of income (or education) who have taken care of their physiological and security needs can direct their effort (and spend) towards self-actualization. Henry Ford's famous quote 'Why is it that when I ask for a pair of hands there is a brain that comes attached to it?' has never resonated so strongly in our organizations. The reasoning goes something like this: customers with low levels of disposable income have little discretionary spend and therefore will primarily buy essential products at the lowest price. The same type of reasoning also applies inside organizations in the form of employees in 'menial' jobs only seek income to meet their basic needs and therefore do not seek the same level of engagement as knowledge workers.

That Maslow's ideas have been used in this way is made all the more ironic when you discover that he rejected the reductive and mechanistic methods of the behaviourists and physiological psychologists of his time.

This misunderstanding renders Maslow's theory useless as an interpretation of the reality of engagement. Look around you; the world is full of exceptions. How many exceptions does it take to make a rule redundant?

Self-actualization is not the preserve of the rich

Let's start with diets. The socio-economic make-up of dieters is varied – poor and rich alike unite in the fight against flab. In his book *The New Marketing Manifesto*, John Grant[3] makes an interesting observation about diets. If Maslow was right, why would people express their self-actualization need (the highest-order need) by starving themselves, thereby rejecting their lowest-order needs? With 7 million US women and 1 million US men suffering from eating disorders, the need to *be someone* is indeed stronger than the need to *be*.[4]

New diets are even more mind-boggling. Food companies now sell branded dieting products (Atkins, Weight Watchers, Slimfast, etc). Thus, not only do poor individuals suppress their physiological needs in order to self-actualize, but many now do so by buying food that is more expensive than the very ingredients whose intake they are trying to suppress!

The same paradox applies in the world of fake goods. In 1982 the International Trade Commission estimated counterfeiting and piracy losses at $5.5 billion. By 1996, that number stood at $200 billion.[5] Why would you want to purchase a fake Armani shirt for more money than it would cost to get a non-branded shirt? The only possible explanation is that your need for identity is satisfied by the brands you wear, but that you do not have enough money for the genuine article. Under Maslow, that does not make much sense.

What about opera? Surely one has to be pretty high up the pyramid before deciding to go to the opera. Why therefore, in 2003, did English National Opera launch its 'tenor for a tenner' initiative to sell tickets for the benefit of lower social classes? The experiment was a resounding success and many opera houses are rushing to follow the example.[6]

The fact is that, in developed economies, most of us have climbed beyond the basic levels of the pyramid, as defined by Maslow. For leaders this carries an important lesson – the pyramid is not quite the shape we thought it was!

Maslow turned upside down

To be successful in engaging customers, leaders need to turn the hierarchy of needs upside down. The need to grow and find meaning is the driver of engagement. Although deficiency needs are still of importance, most Western societies have developed past the point at which these are primary concerns. This is the important distinction; self-actualization remains the primary goal, even when food and water are critical needs. As psychiatrist Viktor E Frankl shows in his book *Man's Search for Meaning*,[7] even during intense periods of deprivation (Frankl's first-hand experience of concentration camps) it is not fulfilling their deficiency needs that keeps people alive but their search for meaning. The affluent societies most of us live in have created a self-actualization vacuum that people are looking to fill whilst the less affluent societies are creating a self-actualization desire that people are struggling, yet strive, to meet.

HOW IS THE NATURE OF ENGAGEMENT CHANGING?

So if the need to engage customers and the search for meaning are not new, then what have Samantha and Michael got to teach us about the changing shape of engagement (at least in an economic sense)? The answer is not in the 'what' but in the 'how'. Samantha and Michael still have the same goal as their forebears, but how they go about meeting that goal has changed.

The end of engagement as we know it

Each generation brings with it new hopes and new beliefs. Each generation sees new possibilities as the world changes and evolves. Just as the steam engine powered the industrial revolution in 19th-century Europe, the search engine powered the 'first world' knowledge revolution of the 20th.

From the industrial age onwards, organizations focused their efforts on manufacturing, and ensuring the consumption of, products. As individuals, we engaged through consumption. First our jobs and then our possessions defined our status. A new series of needs was created by the sheer abundance of new products enabled by increasingly efficient manufacturing processes.

The 'build it and they will buy it' mentality took hold and markets became flooded with ever-more-sophisticated products. The more we produced, the more choices we had. Consequently, it became increasingly difficult to make decisions and achieve satisfaction. As oversupply set in, brands started to become the filters through which customers made choices. Eventually, as individuals became more sophisticated in their relationship with business, they could no longer be satisfied by products alone and moved on to seek new experiences.

The last 10 years have been defined by this thirst for experiences. We no longer engage on the basis of a product alone. Aesthetic design and emotional branding have enabled a more involved relationship with organizations. Yet this relationship is still fundamentally dictated by the organization and relies on a reductive view of individuals, namely as economic agents involved in a transaction. This is inconsistent with Samantha's and Michael's needs.

Why are Samantha and Michael still searching?

As long as our relationship with business was clearly defined and regulated by our roles, there was no problem. We managed to keep our dual 'human doing' (ie employee) and 'human wanting' (ie customer) personalities in check and self-actualize each element of our lives. We built identities through what we did or what we owned.

But the consumption and experience economies carried within them the seed of their own destruction. Driven by the need to offer personal fulfilment, both these economic models encouraged individuals to regain their full identity. Employees became ever more aware of their own value and customers became more aware of their choices. The human 'doing' and 'wanting' disconnect could not exist for long. As individuals take charge of self-actualization outside the confines of their roles (as employees or customers), the organization-dictated experience is no longer fulfilling or sufficient. It is no longer acceptable for individuals to live the organization's vision of what their lives should hold.

The individualistic society

In his book *Bowling Alone*, Harvard's Robert Putman[8] provides plenty of data to demonstrate the changing needs of Samantha and Michael. Armed with a wealth of statistics, Putman looks at the changes in life experiences of different generations. His conclusion is stark and makes one yearn for better, simpler times past. A wide range of indicators (eg membership of political parties, charitable associations, trade unions and religious congregations) indicate that civic engagement has decreased.

In fact, Putman goes on to expand on this notion of community collapse: 'Each generation that has reached adulthood since the 1950s has been less engaged in community affairs than its immediate predecessor.' In conclusion, individuals are more and more alone (hence the title of his book).

So it would seem that, whilst the reality of an individual's need for self-actualization is not changing, at least our relationship with communities and organizations is. No longer are we happy to leave our search for meaning to the mercy of others. Samantha and Michael are now (for better or Putman's worse) in charge.

The disconnect

Putman's work is important because it explains the very roots of the disconnection between people and business. In a world where role boundaries ensured that human 'doings' and 'wantings' knew their place, organizations' engagement tactics ensured an efficient path to a profit-generating transaction. The contractual nature of the relationship was clear and produced transactions.

However, when individuals reconnect with their 'being', these strategies lead to dissonance.

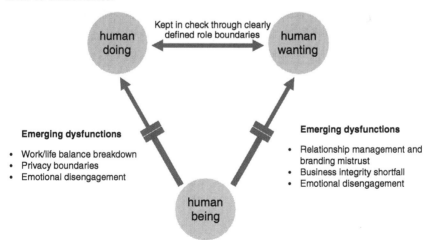

Figure 1.1 Understanding the whole person

Examples of such dissonance abound and are proving a source of constant challenge for today's leaders:

▌ Human beings take offence at working more than living as they search for a definition of who they are that is broader than that of mere economic units. Businesses must learn to connect to human beings, who are neither solely 'doing' nor solely 'wanting'.

▌ The recent increase in spying software on employees' computers as well as data-gathering tools on customers' behaviours would have gone unnoticed in a 'doing'/'wanting' world; in a 'being' world, this is unacceptable and intrusive.

▌ With norms of employment and consumption resembling contractual arrangements, it was well understood by customers and employees that their economic roles entailed acceptance of the organizational desire for control. Today, in a 'being' world, this is widely resented.

▌ The way organizations use data (eg purchase, performance) as a surrogate for knowledge in the building of relationships alienates individuals who desire to 'be' rather than 'want'. Human beings want relationships, and data have never been a substitute for dialogue.

For Samantha and Michael, being reduced to agents in the fulfilment of economic activities will never lead to engagement. The only way to reconnect people and business is to acknowledge, accept and ultimately engage their emotional being.

WHAT ARE THE NEW RULES OF ENGAGEMENT?

So, let's recap. A new reality is forming. As the experience economy comes to pass we are entering Samantha's and Michael's paradoxical world. As they continue to seek ways to achieve their goal of self-actualization, individuals make new demands for engagement:

▌ They are becoming ever more focused on themselves as individuals, yet they cry out for membership of communities.

▌ They want to be secure in deeper relationships, yet they do not want to be dependent.

It is these paradoxes that form the backbone of the new leadership context. We could call this new world the individualistic society (in Putman's honour) but that would be missing the point. Let's call it the people economy and let me explain the point!

The need for communities

In the people economy, providing the means for self-actualization through products, services and jobs is no longer an option. In a world of human beings, organizations become an integral part of the search for meaning.

The way to engage in the people economy is no longer to focus on transactions but, rather, to recognize that these are only of value to people as outcomes of a process of relating. However, to talk about people wanting to engage in relationships, when so many indicators (as Putman's work demonstrated) point to individualism as the norm, warrants some explaining.

That is what makes Samantha and Michael so paradoxical. Why, in a world in which individuals are focused on self-actualization and the search for identity (ie focused on self), would they also be in need of deeper relationships with others?

Wrong type of communities

In his major global study of societal shifts, Ronald Inglehart from the University of Michigan identified changes in society and the demand for engagement[9] in line with what I call the people economy. Individuals' concern for self-actualization is accompanied by a level of demand for engagement in organizational and institutional life that has never been experienced before. But, and here is the crucial part, the fundamental change between community participation pre and post the people economy is in the need for involvement and transparency.

What Putman has defined as a rejection of community life is, in fact, a rejection of old forms of community activities that rely primarily on geographical and role-defined social boundaries (national political parties, local charities and clubs). As this very type of community relies on the acceptance of the human 'wantings' or 'doings' dimensions, it is of little surprise that the old forms could not survive the people economy with its new human beings. That these forms are being rejected (ie that they no longer engage people) is a fact but that doesn't mean that all forms of communities are being rejected. From 1985 to 2000, the number of NGOs increased from 18,000 to 27,898 worldwide.[10] The internet has created an explosion of communities of action (from self-help groups to anarchist movements). 'Non-traditional' political parties (local, one-issue political parties or movements such as the Greens) and direct action groups have witnessed substantial gains in membership.

What individuals in the people economy are rejecting is the notion of communities that rely on authority and hierarchy for their existence. Instead they favour pluralism, diversity and individual contribution. In a world where information has exploded at an exponential rate (the average life of a website is 40 days) the best way to lay down roots, develop trust and therefore build an identity is to create long-lasting relationships by selecting the communities to which you belong. Samantha's and Michael's search for meaning is still dependent on belonging to a community. It's just that theirs doesn't look much like the old one! That's the point of not calling this economy the individualistic society. It isn't individualistic; it's people-centric and relationship focused. The need for communities is as strong as ever. What we, as leaders, must do is understand the new shape of communities. Let me show you how the need for new communities manifests itself and what makes these communities valuable to human beings searching for meaning.

What is communal yearning?

The British Library in London is an imposing building not only because of its architecture; it is an imposing building because of what it stands for. The Library receives a copy of every book published in the UK and Ireland. Each year, the librarians have to add 12 kilometres of linear shelf space in order to accommodate the 3 million new items added to their catalogue. With so many books to read, it's a wonder that any of us still go out and socialize. In fact, if you read five items per day, it would be 80,000 years before you could come out of the imposing red-brick building on London's Euston Road!

While reading is often a solitary occupation, one of the things most librarians talk about today is what they call communal yearning. Communal yearning (the need to construct a community made up of connected individuals) is at the root of the people economy. Libraries, as places of collective memories, form an ideal platform for the creation of communities. Many new libraries not only provide the necessary space for people to meet (cafés and exhibition spaces) but also make a conscious effort to act as hubs for the communities they serve. Bookshops too have become havens of peace for communal encounters. The reason they are ideal for this purpose is that they offer a perfect example of communities where people can, to follow on with Putman's theme, bowl alone yet together. That is to say, they provide a place where people can develop their identity by belonging to a community of like-minded individuals.

Solving the paradox – alone together

These communities are different from the ones Putman laid to rest in that they engage human 'beings', rather than simply fulfilling the needs of human 'wantings' and 'doings'. People economy communities are self-selecting on the basis of their ability to further self-actualization. They are no longer the kind of communities that provided a sense of security in a world where individuals' identities were defined by their role. Just as communities in the Middle Ages were self-selecting, so too are the communities that are forming today, albeit on a larger scale. Milan has become the centre of fashion. Silicon Valley plays host to all things electronic. The free movement of goods, people and ideas has encouraged like-minded individuals to set up relationships. People economy communities form because they help their members pursue their passion. They enable their members to maximize their engagement. They enable people to catch on to the new. Individuals can feed on each other's creativity. This new form of community is prevalent today in the plethora of websites, networks and locations that help people congregate for the sake of their passion. We may listen to our music alone, shutting the world out by putting on the headphones of our MP3 players, but we exchange our files on the web hoping to belong to a community of value.

Communities of engagement

It is these communities that provide engagement. The important thing for leaders to realize is that self-selecting communities can be formed by using interventions that foster a sense of belonging and of unique purpose, in a disparate group. Communities can be engineered.

For this to happen, businesses must create a common goal. Even with a focus on individual activities, people's search for identity is best served by communities. These provide the climate of trust that enables people to create their identity and invest their energy in their search for self-actualization. The reason communal yearning is an important differentiator in the people economy is because this ensures engagement by encouraging belonging.

Community engagement as a process of co-creation

The key to engineering this kind of community is to understand that for it to be attractive to individuals searching for meaning the membership must entail an exchange. As we saw earlier, individuals in the process of defining their identity will not be satisfied with this being defined on their behalf by the organization. People economy individuals empathize with the Prisoner, the character from the iconic 1960s television series, when he cried 'I am not a number.'

If individuals are to use their relationships with communities (of which organizations are an integral part) to define who they are, they will always demand to be involved in the creation process. This is at odds with what organizations and their leaders feel their roles are about. Often, organizations and leaders feel that the creation of products and services is an intricate process for which specialist knowledge must precede engagement. Contemplating co-creation in such an environment would be nonsensical.

So before we turn in the next chapter to how we can build businesses that resemble the kind of communities that engage people, let me close this chapter on the main driver of value in the people economy communities. If we get that right, we have cracked the paradox. Let me introduce you to someone who co-creates in a highly specialist field.

Co-creating a symphony

Seeing Maria Schneider take control of an orchestra shatters once and for all any preconceptions and stereotypes one might have about conductors.[11] In a world where it remains unusual to find a female soloist, finding a female conductor of her stature is rare. However, Maria is not just a conductor – she is also a composer. What makes her relevant to a discussion on co-creation is that Maria has managed to transform what is possibly the most personal act of creation (ie the composition of music) into a complete exchange with a community of individuals (ie her listeners).

First, let's be clear: Maria is not some reclusive fringe composer. That she is successful is beyond argument. Her debut recording, *Evanescence*, was nominated for two 1995 Grammy Awards. Her second and third recordings, *Coming About* and *Allégresse*, were also both nominated for Grammy Awards. Maria has received numerous awards for Best Composer and Best Arranger and one for Best Big Band. Her third album, *Allégresse*, was chosen by both *Time* and *Billboard* magazines in their 'Top Ten recordings of 2000', which was inclusive of all genres of music. However, it is her most recent recording that I want to focus on here, *Concert in the Garden*, which received a Grammy Award in 2005. It is of particular interest because it is the first recording to receive the award without being distributed in record stores.

Co-creation of individual meaning

The way Maria funded her latest recording was by persuading her listeners to contribute to her creative process. Instead of just buying a recorded CD, they engaged with Maria from the start of the creation process. They paid not just to hear her music, but also to gain insights into the creation process. Buying membership into Maria's 'artist exchange' community provided access to her thoughts, her views on what she was doing, pieces especially recorded without the soloists so you could play every solo you wanted, and scores for each piece so you could practise and change them – classical jazz karaoke-style! In this way, Maria created a community of artists (each with different levels of interest) who funded not only her passion but also their own. By buying into the community, individuals also bought into a co-creation of meaning.

Product and services versus meaning and identity

Co-creation of meaning is different from product or service co-creation in that it requires organizational activities to be shared. Both the consumption and experience economies rely on organizations to generate the idea, create the product and experience, and execute. By doing so, they limit their stakeholders' involvement to capital, data or labour provision (thus creating the 'disconnects' identified earlier). You see, for an organization to become a community in which Samantha and Michael search for meaning, they will need to be engaged and involved in idea generation and creation at a deeper level than simply through the provision of data and information. Table 1.1 describes the key distinctions between these economies.

The next step

So, once again, let's recap. In the people economy, the only way to engage individuals is by helping them self-actualize through a community of value. To make any community a community of value, there must be a process of co-creation.

This has major implications for the way we think about our organizations. Co-creation brings with it the possibility of a clash between the organizational and individual agenda. Yet, organizational performance depends on individual engagement that necessitates co-creation. Yet how do you secure the delivery of results against a set of organizational accountabilities defined by roles when the construct of roles is counterproductive in securing engagement in the people economy? How do you ensure that the relationships people want also lead to the transactions organizations need?

These are difficult constructs when applied to organizations that over the last hundred years have become fine-tuned machines. It is hard for leaders, who have always viewed their primary task as the minimization of uncertainty and deviations from plans, to embrace the inherent risks of co-creation. Difficult it may be, necessary it sure is but impossible it isn't. In Chapter 2, I want to introduce you to Torsten. He can help!

THE 30-SECOND RECAP

Engaging customers means being able to help them fulfil their self-actualization goal (ie their search for meaning and identity). Whilst we are all aware of Maslow's hierarchy of needs, we make a mistake when we think of self-actualization as the end of a motivational sequence. The primary goal of human beings, irrespective of social and economic position, is the search for meaning.

Table 1.1 Value creation in the three economies

	Consumption	Experience	People
Drivers of Value	Fulfilling wants/needs through products.	Fulfilling wants and increasing needs through experiences.	Search for meaning and identity through relationships.
Idea Generation	The responsibility of the organization generated by its understanding of what it sees as fit-for-purpose products.	The responsibility of the organization primarily through research contacts with consumers and information exchange with suppliers.	Co-created by users through deep relationships.
Product and Services Creation	Defined by the organization's internal resources.	Defined by the organization's marketing department with involvement from the organization's network.	Resulting from ideas gathered by the customer through own network of experience and providers.
Execution	Organization based.	Organization and supplier network based.	Individuals' network based.

The ways that people fulfil this goal are changing. No longer do they find meaning by virtue of their role alone, or by the products and services they select. The way people now seek to create meaning is by engaging in relationships within communities (of which organizations are part). However, the communities they select are different from the communities that we are used to. People are rejecting communities based on roles and rules, preferring instead communities that help them co-create.

People no longer see transactions as important in themselves. Instead, they view these as the outcome of a process of relating. Relating in this context means taking part in the act of co-creation with organizations. This requires involving people, as human beings (rather than human 'doings' or 'wantings'), in the activities of the organization and will therefore require a new mindset. That new context is what I call the people economy.

This presents a challenge to leaders, as co-creating means not knowing the outcome of the activity at its onset. This is something undesirable for leaders who have always seen risks and deviations from plans as undesirable.

THE LEADERSHIP TAKEAWAY

Here are the points from Chapter 1 that are pertinent to the way you think about leadership:

1. *Motivation exists in everyone – it is your job to find it.*

   - Every healthy human being is motivated and engaged. Humans possess energy that they will allocate to any task provided it is closely aligned to their goals. As leaders it is our job to tap into that energy by understanding what drives each and every one of our stakeholders.
   - Whilst needs are complex and varied, the goal of all human beings is to self-actualize.

2. _Your organization is a community of individuals looking to co-create, not a collection of human resources waiting to deliver._

- In order to self-actualize, people are seeking to reconnect with their humanity (rather than just playing the roles of customer or employee) and fulfil themselves through the relationships they form within communities. That engagement is achieved through a process of co-creation.
- To treat people as resources (human resources in the case of employees and data in the case of customers) who play a part in the creation of a product or a service diminishes the level of engagement possible. It is the role of the leader to build organizations that provide the opportunity for individuals to be involved in the creation of meaning.

2

How do organizations respond?

With his cropped blond hair, jeans, converse trainers and black T-shirt bearing a skull, one wouldn't expect Torsten Schilling to be a golfer, never mind the captain of a 150,000-member-strong golf club. Actually, Torsten is not so much a captain as an organizer. His club is not your typical golf club either – it has no membership cards, no clubhouse and no founding charter. In fact, apart from a website, it has none of the elements that define a club.

A television producer who found himself spending too much time on the road, Torsten started hitting golf balls in hotel corridors. Then, partly because of complaints from hotel managers and partly because of the lack of challenge offered by long, carpeted straight lines, he created Natural Born Golfers (NBG), a club devoted to 'cross-golf' (X-Golf). The idea behind X-Golf is simple: every terrain you encounter, from hotel corridors to building sites, is a potential course – you play wherever you want. You choose a hole (an old bucket or a rusty paint can) and hit the ball.

Torsten's world might seem far removed from yours. You may think that a community of golfers, who according to the Royal and Ancient Golf Club 'aren't real golfers', has little to teach leaders in the corporate world. Think again. Through his efforts, Torsten could be in the process of addressing one of the major challenges faced by leaders in today's people economy: how do you create an organization agile enough to embrace the co-creation needs of self-actualizing customers?

The questions this chapter will answer

▌ How do organizations and individuals become disconnected?

▌ What does an organization designed for engagement look like?

HOW DO ORGANIZATIONS AND INDIVIDUALS BECOME DISCONNECTED?

In Chapter 1 we saw how the people economy necessitates engagement. The network of relationships people build as human beings (rather than just employees or customers) helps them derive meaning and identity. This creates two problems:

▌ Relationships with people economy communities rely on co-creation. Co-creation is only possible if every part of the organization can support it (ie customers do not want to co-create with each and every function). This necessitates the building of strong connections between each part of the organization.

▌ Relationships alone seldom pay the organizational bills. Transactions are ultimately the lifeblood of the corporation. Activities that do not lead to profitable exchange are of little value to any business. Furthermore, relationships that are not based on organizational accountabilities (ie the fulfilment of an organizational need by people) are at best a potential distraction.

The people economy therefore creates a challenge for leaders to resolve. On the one hand the only way to maximize performance is to maximize your share of discretionary effort (or spend) by focusing on relationships. Yet relationships are not, on their own, what will ensure the maximization of performance!

Many organizations manage this clash of purpose through rules and roles. Relationships are created in role silos and follow strict rules in the form of accountabilities. In the people economy, this is counterproductive, as human beings reject regulatory frameworks whose purpose is to maximize transactions. Indeed, these very rules reinforce the lack of connections between each function (ie as each is given specific accountabilities to fulfil) that are necessary for co-creation.

Riding around dirt tracks on their Harley-Davidson golf carts, Torsten and his NBG army are finding a new way to reconcile the demand for transactions with the need for relationships. Here is how they do it and what their example tells us.

The failure to engage

Just like any leader, Torsten relies on transactions for NBG to be successful. In his case the transaction is a game of golf. There is little point in having a golf club if you can't have a golf game. All players need to fulfil their accountabilities. Without the fulfilment of accountabilities by role holders – be they customer or employee roles – organizations cannot survive. What makes X-Golf interesting in the context of the 'transaction versus relationship' problem becomes apparent when you contrast this to 'traditional' golf.

In order to cope with technological and societal changes, golf (like all other human endeavour) has suffered from an exponential increase in regulations. Indeed, golf has gone from having 13 rules (comprising a total of 338 words) in 1744, to 132 pages' worth (nearly 40,000 words) in 2003.[1] The problem with rules and roles is that they do not constitute the basis of engagement in the people economy. In Chapter 1 we have seen how psychologically, as self-actualization emerges, the relationship with the community evolves from a state of dependence (ie you need the community in order to know who you are) to one of interdependence (both the community and you are dependent on each other for definition). People are actively rejecting rule-based communities as places of engagement.

The problem with organizations

Yet, like golf, for the last 100 years our organizations have followed quite a predictable evolution. In the late 1880s, Richard Sears, an agent for the Minneapolis and St Louis railway in Minnesota, purchased a job lot of watches. He began selling them to colleagues up and down the railway track. The business proved popular and eventually, in 1886, Richard set up the RW Sears Watch Company in Minneapolis and put out his first recruitment advert.

The Sears story is a classic story of US retail – one founder with a deep understanding of his customers, passion and a breakthrough idea. It is also a classic example of the problem with organizations having to respond to the challenges of the people economy.

Making big small

But 19th-century Sears was small. To thrive, Richard Sears knew he had to grow. Yet, he also knew, as many of his managers would later discover, that being small gave him an advantage. Being small meant that he always knew what was going on. He could spot opportunities and problems and was sufficiently agile to make things happen quickly.

To gain the opportunities afforded by being big without losing the advantages of being small, Richard Sears and his managers took the route many have taken previously and since – they made being big feel smaller. They broke the organization into its component parts and put in place levels of control. By concentrating most of its buying and decision-making power in centralized functions located in its Chicago headquarters, Sears could ensure that it exploited its size to the full.

Built on hierarchical decomposition and structural reduction, Sears, like many other organizations, defined everything: jobs, accountabilities, departments, etc – all the preconditions necessary for control. Organizations as we know them are primarily instruments of control engineered to overcome the issues of size. They need rules to operate. I call this type of organization 'the formal'.

Roles take centre stage

The 'formal' is by definition designed. What Newton did for physics, Taylor embraced for work and Sloan adapted for management. Once the organization has been created, it aims to collect as many data as possible in order to remove discrepancies from plan to action. The resulting predictive models define anything unplanned as undesirable. In the 'formal' Sears, everything follows strict, clear role definitions:

▌ The supplier's role is to supply raw material at the lowest-possible cost with minimal variance in quality and time.

▌ The employee's role is to conform and obey all rules with minimal variance in competence against a predetermined model of 'perfect role-person motivational fit'.

▌ The consumer's role is to buy, and preferably consume, with minimal variance in taste.

As the dehumanizing process takes place, rules become the primary driver of performance. In this context, the leader's role is to control the creation process by providing direction in the form of a strategy and the means to achieve it in the form of a plan. Resources (human or otherwise) need to be aligned.

Organizations and change

When Frederick Brooks said 'nine women can't make a baby in one month',[2] he might not have known that he was foreseeing the downfall of the 'formal' organization. It doesn't matter how many times you divide a task or how many resources you throw at it, the complexity associated with creation does not obey the rules of analytical deconstruction. The deconstructed human being (ie wanting and doing) only provides limited resources in an engagement-intensive people economy. When the organizational chart becomes overcrowded with boxes and lines (straight, twisted, solid and dotted), everything becomes complicated. Unless the organization can operate cross-functionally, customers' co-creation needs will go unanswered. But organizations do evolve and have evolved.

The new formal

Contrast Sears with the retail behemoth Wal-Mart and it would seem we have come a long way since the days of over-regulation.

Sam Walton's creation is an amazing success however you define it. Not only does it sell more than Sears, but it sells more than Sears, K-Mart, Safeway, JC Penney and Kroger combined. With $256 billion in annual sales, it sells in three months what its US number 2, Home Depot, sells in a year. It is three times the size of the French retail giant Carrefour. Its revenues generate a mind-boggling 2.3 per cent of US GDP.

Of course, such scale is not unknown. Sears itself represented 1 per cent of US GDP in the early 1980s. What has never been witnessed before, however, is Wal-Mart's ability to combine agility with scale. How can a company that remains true to only one fundamental value – driving down prices – manage to be so extraordinarily resilient to attacks in the form of changes in customer tastes?

In Sam we trust

From the start, Sam Walton set out to build an organization that can only be defined as one long customer satisfaction process. His idea was simple – design an organization that is not only structured for execution (as Sears was, with deep hierarchies and functions), but also agile enough to ensure creation with well-defined yet highly flexible processes.

Wal-Mart devolves decision-making power to the point closest to the customer but, unlike Sears, it does so without retaining control. Store managers enjoy more flexibility than in any other retail environment. They can try out new ideas in their stores (a bold move when you consider the premium put on shelf space in any retail business) and, if such an idea works well, processes ensure the new local practice becomes global best practice.

The now mythical Sam, in his book *Made in America*, talks about his 10 rules for building a business in terms that could not be found in a 'formal' organization's dictionary – 'Remain a corporation and retain control if you like, but behave as a servant leader in a partnership', 'Communicate everything you possibly can to your partners', 'Money and ownership alone aren't enough', 'Constantly, day by day, think of new and more interesting ways to motivate and challenge your partners [Wal-Mart's word for employees].'[3] In fact, of the 10 rules, at least nine have to do with ways of dealing with people (customers, suppliers and employees).

Wal-Mart's success can be explained by two words that are, on the face of it, contradictory – consistency and flexibility. Wal-Mart has an in-built consistency in terms of its direction (execute at the lowest-possible cost) mixed with a passion for flexibility in meeting customer needs (create new services and products that can adapt quickly to local market conditions).

Consistently inconsistent

Could this be the kind of community that would appeal to Samantha and Michael? Like X-Golf, it seems that Wal-Mart is designed to fulfil the need of its stakeholders. Mix mass with velocity and you get momentum. Mix Wal-Mart's incredible mass with its incredible velocity and you get unparalleled momentum. With 21,000 suppliers providing products to the 140 million people who are served every week by its 1.5 million employees, Wal-Mart recognizes the need to think holistically about the organization's system. With so much going on, working cross-functionally, whilst necessary, must be difficult. To ensure it happens, Wal-Mart has replaced structures with processes.

So, is Wal-Mart an organization built for resilience in the face of customers' changing needs? Has Wal-Mart found a way of marrying transactions with relationships, enabling it to weather the people economy storm?

Wal-Mart will fail unless it changes

In fact, just like Sears before it, Wal-Mart is now struggling with context change. No longer can it be said to be the darling of business analysts it once was. Just as with Sears before it, it is the people economy that is pitted against Wal-Mart's inherent demand to optimize returns at the point of transaction. Whilst processes might help face the challenge of connections, the challenge of transactions versus relationships is not helped by processes alone.

Wal-Mart has not been exempt from criticism when it comes to the way it leads in its markets. Whilst it rejects the charges made against it, the organization was sufficiently hurt by mounting suspicion to launch a US-wide advertising campaign in January 2005 that was intended to counter the charges.

Wal-Mart has come under pressure, accused of paying wages to some of its partners that are below the official federal poverty line. It has had applications for new stores blocked by some city councils fearing damage to local communities. One supplier to Wal-Mart was quoted as saying 'There is only one thing worse than doing business with Wal-Mart and that may well be not doing business with Wal-Mart.'[4] Despite this, a few have stopped working with the giant, believing that, since the fat in the supply chain had already been cut, they risked losing their hearts. Wal-Mart executives have even come under pressure in the off-shoring debate, as suppliers are said to be exporting US jobs in order to reduce costs further to fulfil their commitment to the giant.[5]

In fact, the New York City Pension Fund, worth $85 billion, and Illinois's State Board of Investment have written to Wal-Mart executives asking for internal controls to be tightened. They fear the 'potential contingent liabilities and negative effects on the company's stock price and reputation' arising from regulatory breaches.[6]

The more things change...

Only on the face of it does Wal-Mart offer an alternative to Sears' Taylorism. There is no doubt that an organization acknowledging both the human and the system dimensions of the enterprise becomes more agile. However, despite the changes Sam Walton endeavoured to make, Wal-Mart and other process-centric organizations still fundamentally create value through roles and their separation along manageable lines of control. It is that reality that stops an organization being connected enough to be a community of value in people economy terms:

▌ Suppliers, although closer to the organization, are only integrated through technology as a source of competitive advantage.

▌ A powerful combination of alignment and empowerment now ensures that the human resource makes the right choices, but we still need a copious dose of conformity and control to align people to key processes.

▌ Customers still have to be made to realize that the product or service is the answer to a need they didn't know they had. They are now targeted through consultative selling, helped by data from customer relationship management systems that enable the organization to offer to a more relevant population.

Wal-Mart has not created a new type of organization; it has simply put the 'formal' on steroids. This 'new formal' still creates value through transactions between roles. In the 'formal' organization, there is no value in relationships other than in so far as they help make transactions happen. In this context, with businesses on a path to alignment, individuals driven by a sense of identity can only leave their humanity outside the walls of the corporation, looking in. Table 2.1 outlines the similarities and differences between old and new formal organizations.

John Maynard Keynes, the famed economist, commenting on the potential impact of long-term monetary policy, once wrote: 'in the long run we're all dead'! Unfortunately, if asked what the impact of rules and control on organizational success will be, the same answer applies.

Rules, roles and rewards

But to say that organizations depend on rules and controls alone is an oversimplification. Any organization, NBG included, actually relies on two key mechanisms to ensure that things happen: rules are one and incentives the other – in other words, the proverbial sticks and carrots.

So, let's get back to NBG. Unlike traditional golf, NBG has only two rules: 'Be safe' and 'Have fun.' The community is fundamentally constructed on relationships. There is an elegant simplicity in the nature of the relationship between the business (NBG) and its members. Participants in NBG are fully engaged in an effort to ensure that the transaction happens. The

Table 2.1 Creating value in the formal and new formal

	Formal	New Formal
Focus	Consistency in delivery of core offering. Executing to defend, extend and increase profitability of existing business.	Agility initiatives to respond to change or build new business.
Layer Purpose		
Input	Control through functional structure. Clearly defined economic roles.	Response through process. Clearly defined economic roles within an integrated process.
– Supplier Role	Supply at lowest-possible cost.	Integrate through technology to maximize flexibility and supply at lowest-possible cost.
– Customer Role	Purchase at price.	Share information to tailor product and services and purchase at price.
– Employee Role	Conform and obey.	Contribute and align.
Output	Annual operating plans, tactical plans, budgets.	Business change-building strategies, investment budgets, detailed business plans for change ventures, organization values.
Financial Focus	Near bottom-line results and cash flow.	Top-line growth and capital productivity.
Economic Measures	Planned profit achievement. Return on capital invested. Costs. Productivity and efficiency. EVA.	Revenue growth. Market share or installed base, MVA. New customer acquisitions. Profit capital invested efficiencies. Expected NPV.

founder and members share a common purpose, which they together strive to achieve.

This observation was also true of Sears and Wal-Mart in the early days. As we saw, the challenge faced by growing organizations is to make big feel small. Leaders only use rules as they aim to keep organizational purpose alive in a group that is growing ever more complex and more physically and emotionally distant from its founders. At the stage at which they do so, their organizations make the switch from 'purpose in search of assets' to 'assets in search of purpose'. When leaders say 'Think customers', employees will hear 'Think transaction.'

The failure of incentives to engage

The reason this happens has less to do with the nature of rules and more to do with the nature of incentives. This was brought home to me by my eight-year-old daughter. A few months ago, Charlotte decided that she wanted pocket money. In the eager parenting spirit of treating every opportunity as a learning opportunity, Charlotte, her mother and I discussed and agreed that she could have pocket money if she earned it! An incentive scheme was duly designed.

For brushing her hair and teeth every day Charlotte would earn 10p. For doing her homework, she would earn 40p (why teeth should be cheaper than education was, in itself, a matter of debate). Tidying her bedroom would earn her 10p. For not shouting at her brother (the obligatory stretch target) she would earn 10p, etc.

One Saturday (the evening before payday), I reminded Charlotte of the need to tidy her bedroom. She went upstairs. Fifteen minutes later, silence prevailed. As any parent knows, 15 minutes of silence is never a good sign. I went upstairs to measure progress. I opened the bedroom door only to find as much mess as had been there before Charlotte had gone up. Charlotte was lying on her bed, painting her nails with her finest Barbie nail varnish.

I decided to keep my cool in confronting Charlotte's behaviour and only asked 'When will you tidy the bedroom?' Her reply told me everything I needed to know about the problem with economic incentives. 'You see, Papa, I think that, for 10 pence, tidying just isn't worth it!' If wanting Charlotte to learn the meaning of money had been the objective, then the objective would have been exceeded – I was now bargaining with my own daughter. I half-expected her to refer me to her union representative!

The need for moral and social obligations

Colleagues who specialize in incentive schemes tell me that the experience highlights the most basic rule of incentives: 'The receiver's perception of the value of the prize has to be proportionate to his or her perception of the effort needed to get it.'

Yet, the lesson I decided to take away is not that incentive plans need to be better designed. Rather, the lesson of importance here is that economic incentives actively destroy moral and social obligation – Charlotte will no longer conduct a task unless it is stated in the list of accountabilities measured by the remuneration programme.

The only way to get Charlotte's full performance (ie her positive engagement with the task accompanied by the release of her discretionary effort) and ensure context resilience (ie get performance even if asking people to do something unforeseen at the time of drafting their account-abilities) is to build something greater than the economic incentive.

Incentives to encourage transactions ensure that the moral or social obligation to the customer comes second. The reliance on rules minimizes moral or social obligations. Yet the type of communities that individuals in the people economy are looking for are ones based on these obligations rather than regulatory frameworks.

Creating a different kind of community

To build its community, NBG uses a different type of incentive. NBG maximizes co-creation opportunities by minimizing rules. The reason it requires less rules than other organizations is because it relies on a different kind of incentive to ensure engagement. The kind of incentive it relies on is the very kind of incentive that people economy communities thrive on.

Economists talk about three basic kinds of incentives:

▌ *Economic incentives.* You do something because there is an economic gain in doing it.

▌ *Social incentives.* You do something because it is consistent with the expectations of a community to which you want to belong.

▌ *Moral incentives.* You do something because you feel it is morally right to do so.

It is that mix of incentives with a primary focus on social and moral obligations that enables NBG to maximize the release of discretionary effort whilst ensuring transactions happen.

Wanting + doing = cheating

It is reliance on economic incentives over social and moral obligations that leads to a need for an overbearing regulatory framework. As social and moral obligations are removed and the focus instead becomes the maximization of the economic incentive, we end up with the biggest disconnects of all.

Regulatory frameworks and economic incentives make it permissible for members of a community (no longer tied by moral or social obligations) to cheat. For businesses in the people economy this means that transactions are not maximized, as relationships become a secondary concern to the meeting of economic targets.

The same regulatory framework, in turn, creates the illusion of loyalty and customer engagement. Take loyalty cards as an example. If these worked, why do I have four in my wallet (one for each of the supermarkets at which I shop)? Why do I try to maximize the amount of free air miles from my airline by complaining about the slightest delay in the hope of a discretionary compensatory award? Loyalty schemes are not loyalty schemes at all. Loyalty is based on an intricate system of moral and social obligations, whilst 'loyalty' schemes are based on economic incentives. Engaged in an economic battle for bribery with most businesses, like Charlotte, I firmly intend to win.

Purpose versus rules

When communities such as NBG rely on social and moral incentives as their primary carrots, people fulfil accountabilities (as suppliers, employees and customers) because they want to do so and feel it is right to do so. They go the extra mile to ensure the purpose is fulfilled, thereby creating communities to which they want to belong. They create the connections between customers and organizations necessary to the fulfilling of customer needs.

Economic incentives, on the other hand, sub-optimize engagement because they remove humanity by concentrating on the human 'wanting' or 'doing' dimensions alone. Subjected to ever-increasing controls and rules to regulate transactions, individuals forget what it is that made them want to take part in the game in the first place, other, that is, than the economic incentives.

To encourage the release of effort through social and moral obligations and thereby ensure the whole organization is invested in the co-creation of meaning with its stakeholders, NBG needs to encourage its members to co-create the game. Co-creation, as we saw in Chapter 1, is a key to success in the people economy. It creates a virtual cycle by building stronger communities with a stronger sense of social and moral obligations. Driven (no golf pun intended) by purpose, enthusiasts find each other, build communities and fulfil accountabilities for the sake of a common agenda. It is the process of co-creation that leads to the connection being powerful. In the case of NBG, it is the dialogue that accompanies decisions on how the game will be played that leads to engagement.

WHAT DOES AN ORGANIZATION DESIGNED FOR ENGAGEMENT LOOK LIKE?

The story of organization development as exemplified by Sears and Wal-Mart is, in fact, one of economic incentives run amok. In the people economy, creating moral and social obligations (ie creating the type of communities described in Chapter 1) is critical to success.

Reciprocity

Social and moral obligations are best described as reciprocity. In order to work, any free human system relies primarily on reciprocity (mutual give and take). Reciprocity acts as the vector in networks, giving a sense of direction to individuals' efforts as they engage with a common purpose.

Reciprocity is not the same as egocentricity or conformity (ie the behaviours required for the successful fulfilment of an economic incentive), nor does it need to be immediate. I may lend you a pen because I know that sometime in the future, if I ever need a pen, you will probably lend one to me. I may give to charity to help the homeless. I don't do this, however, because I might some day benefit from my investment. Rather, I do it because I would rather live in a world with less homelessness. By emphasizing the 'why' rather than the 'if-then', reciprocity sets itself apart from economic incentives.

Building real performance contracts

Think about performance management systems that rely on economic incentives and corrective deterrence. Think about the link between targets and pay. Think about most sales strategies devised over the last 20 years and the multiple 'How to close the sale and overcome customer objections' training programmes. And then ask yourself these questions: if your organization's performance management system was abolished, would you stop performing? If laws were unenforceable, which ones would you break?

I scan all my shopping at my local supermarket with a hand-held scanner and pay directly at a special automatic till. Do I steal? No. I pay for my newspaper by putting money in a box to avoid the queue. Do I ever not pay? No. In fact, WH Smith, the retailer that started the honesty box system, says that there is always more money in the box than there should be at the end of the day. It seems that people would rather insert more money when they don't have the right change than pay less than the price of the paper! The reason is a moral and social one. The deterrence of being caught plays little part in my decision. Under a system of reciprocity, far from being passive observers, individuals instead invest in relationships. They respect the norms. For a business, this is critical. Reciprocity means that each and every function, each and every employee, works as one with the customer by being held together by a shared sense of meaning.

The 'formal' organization, with its focus on economic incentives to drive transactions rather than relationships, fails to create reciprocity. It is hard for leaders who fail to recognize humanity to use moral or social incentives. The feeling of obligation individuals feel towards an organization becomes dependent on their own moral and social needs, rather than coming from a sense of obligation nurtured by the organization and individuals as part of an act of co-creation.

Building an organization designed for engagement

A people economy community does not leave the building of such obligations to chance; it actively engineers this. That's it. That's the role of leaders. They must build organizations that rely on obligations to co-create the communities necessary to the fulfilment of people economy customers' needs.

The underlying theme is a form of organization based on horizontal relations of reciprocity – and the behaviours that foster these relationships. This is in contrast to the focus of the 'formal' organization, which emphasizes vertical relations of accountability (ie economic incentives) that, whilst still important, are no longer sufficient.

The 'real' organization

I call this new type of organization the 'real' organization, not only because it does help customers find their reality (ie self-actualization), but also because it is _really_ how things get done in organizations.

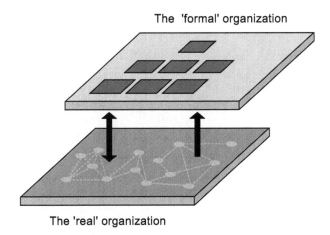

Figure 2.1   A picture of the total organization

To talk about the 'real' organization is to talk about the place where relationships happen. We depend on this 'real' organization. No 'textbook' organization design could possibly work without the informal charts, quiet words, friendships, partnerships, corridor conversations, etc. Relationships between individuals can be represented as connections. Networks of connections take many forms: some are productive, even critical to the task of the organization, others are irrelevant and some may even be destructive.

At their most basic, these networks are groups of connections or interactions that are not hierarchical in form – that is, each node in the network connects to several or many other nodes. The 'formal' organization without the 'real' is an impossibility (everywhere humans co-exist, and the real is present). In stark contrast, a 'formal' organization with a weak, suppressed or counterproductive 'real' layer is a disaster because it counters the building of social and moral incentives. Table 2.2 describes the attributes of the 'real' layer.

Table 2.2   Creating value in the real organization

	Real
Focus	Generation of co-creation opportunities to deepen engagement through community of value.
Layer Purpose	Co-creation through networks.
Input	Networks of connections to ease integration and respond to insights.
– Supplier	Engage in co-creation process driven from compatible unique purpose and help write co-creation script.
– Customer	Orchestrate co-creation.
– Employee	Sense co-creation opportunities and manage co-creation risks.
Output	Business change-building strategies, investment budgets, detailed co-creation plans for change ventures, organization values.
Financial Focus	Size of pay-off and probability of success.
Economic Measures	Project-based milestones. Rate of conversion from idea to co-created business launch. Number of initiatives.

The value of the 'real'

Engaging customers in the people economy is only possible with a 'real' layer that is fully exploited by the leader. The 'real' organization provides agility. This is because the 'real' layer is made up of networks and connections. Networks can take many forms. Computers on the internet are connected into a network. A group of friends who interact equally and socially form a network. A number of functions or colleagues who share best practice without a single central controller are a network. As a network, the 'real' organization has a number of characteristics that make it especially valuable in the people economy.

Fundamentally, it is robust – you cannot destroy a network by removing only one or two nodes. The internet was originally designed as a military communication system that could survive massive loss of nodes in the event of a nuclear attack, by routeing communications around gaps. Compare this with the effect of removing a senior role from a hierarchy as a way to contrast the resilience of 'real' versus 'formal' performance.

A second advantage of the 'real' form of organization lies in its diversity. Typically, a network has many different sorts of interconnections.

Each individual or node is connected to several other nodes. This creates richer conversations and opportunities for co-creation. As a corollary, networks are more flexible than hierarchies – communities of interest form around hot topics and disperse again as required. This helps organizations approach problems differently and solve them more quickly than through the use of 'formal' instruments. The informality, tolerance for ambiguity and agility of the 'real' organization enable it to survive context change.

Networks as the missing connections

It is for these reasons that networks are popular with business leaders – they offer the potential for transfer of innovation and expertise without expensive and distant central coordination. As seen in the Sears example, very often such central coordination destroys local innovation by filtering it through layers of bureaucracy that increase the chances of eventual irrelevance to context change. It is the robust and diverse nature of networks that gives the 'real' organization the flexibility and agility necessary to succeed in the people economy.

However, the benefits of the network can only be realized if it is aligned with the strategic intent of the organization. Torsten still needs a game to happen and his members to respect the two rules. Leaders who do not have a language to describe the 'real' and revert to their 'formal' vocabulary miss the opportunities to align 'formal' with 'real'. As a result, any action they take to engage with the 'real' increases the gap rather than closing it.

Getting real

By focusing on the 'real' organization to achieve formal objectives, leaders must build the social and moral obligations that make people engage and commit to the purpose of the organization. When operating together, the formal and real organizations create the conditions for success by enabling the complete set of core competencies necessary for success:

- an individual interface that is essential to idea generation because it provides the insights necessary for change;

- a set of management processes that ensure the creation of commercially viable propositions (products or services) that in turn deliver the organizational promise;

▌ a delivery system that is flawless in its ability to execute propositions time and time again.

Without a clear focus on all three elements, organizations cannot fulfil their purpose. A sole reliance on economic incentives to deliver the purpose means that the conditions for engagement cannot be created. By concentrating on developing the 'real' organization, leaders can ensure that individuals experience a moral and social obligation towards the fulfilment of the organization purpose as the organization itself becomes a critical part of the individual's network of value (ie it helps the individual create meaning and an identity).

What must leaders do to ensure a healthy 'real' organization? What does securing engagement mean in practice? Four years ago, I met a man who knows and I want to introduce him to you in Chapter 3.

THE 30-SECOND RECAP

Over the last 100 years, organizations have become assets in search of a purpose. Organizations' reliance on rules and economic incentives to counter the problem of size has created a disconnection in an environment in which individuals seek communities in which they can fully invest themselves.

The primary model of today's organizations is one that emphasizes structures and processes. I call this model the 'formal'. Whilst well suited to the delivery of goods and services in the more stable consumption and experience economies, the 'formal' fails to respond to the needs of the people economy. The problem most leaders encounter is their fear that individual and organization purpose will be at odds with each other, leading them to rely on rules and economic incentives to create alignment. This actively destroys engagement in an economy where people want to invest themselves fully.

In order to recapture engagement, leaders must abandon their sole focus on the 'formal' organization and nurture the 'real' organization that lies within their own business. The 'real' organization is the system of informal relationships that enable all organizations to function. It is critical to success in the people economy, as it creates the social and moral obligations that ensure not only individual engagement, but individual engagement targeted at the fulfilment of organization-critical accountabilities. The differences between the 'formal' organization (and its 'new formal' variant) and the 'real' organization are highlighted in Table 2.3.

Table 2.3 Complete and sustainable value creation

	Formal	New Formal	Real
Focus	Consistency in delivery of core offering. Executing to defend, extend and increase profitability of existing business.	Agility initiatives to respond to change or build new business.	Generation of co-creation opportunities to deepen engagement through community of value.
Purpose	Control through functional structures.	Response through process.	Co-creation through networks.
Input	Clearly defined economic roles.	Clearly defined economic roles with integrating processes.	Networks of connections to ease integration and respond to insights.
– Supplier	Supply at the lowest cost.	Integrate through technology to maximize flexibility and supply at lowest-possible cost.	Engage in co-creation process driven from compatible unique purpose and help write co-creation script.
– Customer	Purchase at price.	Share information to tailor product and service and purchase at price.	Orchestrate co-creation.
– Employee	Conform and obey.	Contribute and align.	Sense co-creation opportunities and manage co-creation risks.

(Continued on next page)

Table 2.3 (*Continued*)

	Formal	New Formal	Real
Output	Annual operating plans, tactical plans and budgets.	Business change-building strategies, investment budgets, detailed business plans for change ventures, organization values.	Prototypes and trials, communications and strategic co-creation, milestones plans.
Financial Focus	Near bottom-line results and cash flow.	Top-line growth and capital productivity.	Size of pay-off and probability of success.
Economic Measures	Planned profit achievement. Return on capital invested. Costs. Productivity and efficiency. EVA.	Revenue growth. Market share or installed base, MVA. Profit capital invested efficiencies. Expected NPV.	Project-based milestones. Rate of conversion from idea to co-created business launch. Number of initiatives.

THE LEADERSHIP TAKEAWAY

Here are the points from Chapter 2 that are pertinent to the way you think about leadership:

3. *Bribery is no longer a performance management option.*

   – For the last 100 years, organizations have been built on systems of economic incentives (ie performance or purchase carried an economic reward). Economic incentives are not only open to abuse but, by removing the moral and social obligations placed on individuals, they actually encourage cheating (ie sub-optimized relationships).
   – To mitigate this, leaders use rules and defined roles. Unfortunately such reliance on rules and roles directly contributes to organizations' inability to succeed in the people economy because, as we saw in Chapter 1, individuals in the people economy no longer accept communities based on roles and rules alone.

4. *Focus on relationships not structures.*

   – Leaders must therefore focus their effort on helping customers release their full humanity as opposed to just fulfil their role accountabilities. This alone will lead to engagement.
   – In the people economy humanity is released in networks of trust (ie communities based on social and moral obligations rather than rules). These networks form the 'real' organization (ie the way people get things done and why they do them).
   – Your role is to ensure that these communities are created by focusing your effort not on creating formal structures but on helping the 'real' organization (ie the networks of value-added relationships currently happening informally in your business) to be expressed and aligned to your organization's formal objectives.

Diagnostic tools 1:

Do you know what people want?

HOW READY ARE YOU FOR THE PEOPLE ECONOMY?

The following questions will help you reflect on the shift your organization has experienced in terms of its economic focus. Are you capitalizing on the changes brought about by the people economy or are you still looking back at the consumption or experience economies?

On each of the following scales (from 1 to 11) circle the number that best represents where you are with respect to your relationships with your stakeholders.

	Consumption		Experience	People
	Developed internally	Consultation with suppliers	Consultation with customers	Developed jointly

1. Drivers of value

• Needs assessment	1	2	3	4	5	6	7	8	9	10	11
• Product service	1	2	3	4	5	6	7	8	9	10	11
• Experience	1	2	3	4	5	6	7	8	9	10	11
• Price	1	2	3	4	5	6	7	8	9	10	11

2. Idea generation

• Future visioning	1	2	3	4	5	6	7	8	9	10	11
• Knowledge of what is possible	1	2	3	4	5	6	7	8	9	10	11
• Research and development	1	2	3	4	5	6	7	8	9	10	11
• Information gathering	1	2	3	4	5	6	7	8	9	10	11
• Product usage strategy	1	2	3	4	5	6	7	8	9	10	11

3. Product/service creation

• Product development plans	1	2	3	4	5	6	7	8	9	10	11
• Product design	1	2	3	4	5	6	7	8	9	10	11
• User testing	1	2	3	4	5	6	7	8	9	10	11
• Feedback gathering	1	2	3	4	5	6	7	8	9	10	11
• Quality benchmarking	1	2	3	4	5	6	7	8	9	10	11

4. Execution

• Costing	1	2	3	4	5	6	7	8	9	10	11
• Pricing	1	2	3	4	5	6	7	8	9	10	11
• Selling	1	2	3	4	5	6	7	8	9	10	11
• Distribution	1	2	3	4	5	6	7	8	9	10	11
• Marketing	1	2	3	4	5	6	7	8	9	10	11

Interpreting your results

Assuming that each of the activities above carries an equal value you can draw the following conclusions:

▌ If you score less than 70, you are still operating from the inside out. This consumption mindset means that you have to place more emphasis on your leaders being right about the future direction of the market you operate in that is appropriate in the current climate. You must develop strategies to be closer to your suppliers in order to build some agility.

▌ If you score from 70 to 150, you have already developed some of the dynamics that enable you to provide a consistent experience and bring outside influences into your organization. It is nevertheless essential for future resilience to capitalize on these early successes and look for further and deeper co-creation opportunities with your customers.

▌ If you score more than 150, your operating model is firmly rooted in the people economy. Your challenge is to ensure that your role continues to be one of coordinating the internal and external influences.

Next steps

In a different colour, you may want to circle the number that best represents where you think your organization aspires to be. If there is a difference, it indicates a need to accelerate or create plans to close the gap. Where there is no gap, it is worth asking others to check your answers against their perception, as maybe you need to rethink your perception of what success looks like.

Try to think through the same exercise with your competitors in mind. Are their results similar to yours? Does this mean that there is an opportunity in the industry for a new type of relationship with stakeholders or does it simply reflect the reality of the sector you operate in?

Moving your operating model from the consumption to the people economy relies in part on changing the focus of your organization away from internal operations to outside influences. Chapter 2 showed how this is largely done by understanding the different layers of the organization and focusing equally on each of the component parts. The exercise below will help you diagnose your modus operandi as a leader.

IS YOUR ORGANIZATION A 'REAL' COMMUNITY?

The following set of questions will help you reflect on your organization focus. What your organization values and encourages will either unlock the potential of your 'real' layer or maximize the emphasis on 'formal' instruments.

Which of the attributes below does your organization encourage and reward? Rank all of the attributes below with 1 being the attributes perceived as the least rewarded and encouraged and 9 the attributes perceived as the most rewarded and encouraged (write these scores in the Ranking boxes).

This is about your employees' reality rather than your strategic intent (ie it doesn't matter what you think you try to do; what matters is the signals your employees experience regarding what is valued). Therefore try to answer these as if you were on the receiving end of your leadership.

Ranking

1. Team work across work units

2. Building strategic alliances with other organizations

3. Being highly organized

4. Responding to customer feedback

5. Minimizing unpredictability

6. Increasing decision-making speed by devolving it

7. Maximizing customer satisfaction

8. Using resources outside the company to get things done

9. Maintaining clear lines of accountability and authority

Now add together the numbers for each attribute as shown below:

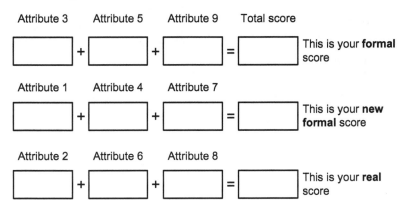

Your highest score will show you where your employees feel your main area of focus is. Even though this is a very limited set of questions, their reality will tend to dictate the nature of their action.

In the people economy, we clearly need to reconnect the reality experienced inside the organization with the reality felt outside it. Therefore it is worth conducting a similar exercise for stakeholders. What is the reality experienced by your customers? What would they say about your organization? Again, rank the items from 1 to 9 with 1 being what you think would be the least common response from your customers and 9 what you think would be the most common.

Ranking

1. They have all my details in one place and all have access to them.

2. They make it easy for me to consume elsewhere if I need to.

3. They get things right first time.

4. They'll go the extra mile.

5. They are reliable and dependable.

6. When I need something they don't do, I know they will help me find it.

7. They continuously monitor my satisfaction.

8. I feel I am as much part of the organization as they are.

9. If you want something out of the ordinary they will consult their boss.

Again, add together the numbers for each attribute as shown below:

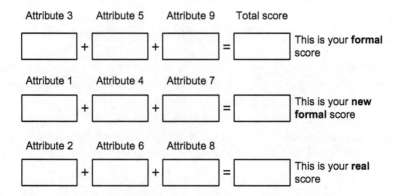

Attribute 3	Attribute 5	Attribute 9	Total score	
+	+	=		This is your **formal** score

Attribute 1	Attribute 4	Attribute 7		
+	+	=		This is your **new formal** score

Attribute 2	Attribute 6	Attribute 8		
+	+	=		This is your **real** score

How does the reality experienced by your customers differ from that of your employees? How can you ensure the two realities align?

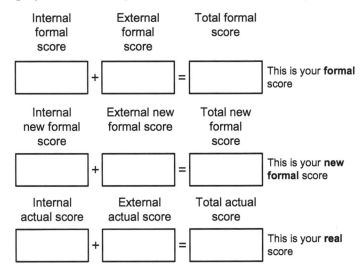

Interpreting your results

Where your focus is does not just indicate preferences; it tells you how resilient your organization is likely to be to context change. Of course, it would be preposterous to argue that an entire organizational strategy can be devised or analysed on the basis of 18 statements. However, based on your answers to the above exercise, the table below shows you some of the profiles of organizations and how this affects their resilience.

For this exercise, a healthy layer would score at least 30 when the internal and external scores are added.

Where is your organization? Can you think of the levers that you need to pull to make all three layers healthy?

Formal	New Formal	Real	Organization Profile
✗	✓	✓	Under siege.
✓	✗	✗	Running out of steam.
✗	✓	✗	Invests new futures but does not capitalize on stakeholders' ability
✗	✗	✓	to make the company future proof.
✓	✗	✓	Generates ideas for the future and executes today but slow to translate ideas into business.
✓	✓	✗	Agile enough for situational change but not context change resilient.

Next steps

Discuss your results with colleagues. Do they have a similar understanding to yours? It is important to recognize that your individual preferences (style of leadership) will impact your perception of what is the right focus to have.

To call an organizational layer healthy is to recognize that it is aligned to the organizational strategy. In the case of the 'real' layer, as we have seen, this alignment cannot be achieved through control and coercion. Part 2 looks at the type of leadership necessary to ensure a balanced approach to making your organization work.

Part Two

The case for connected leadership

Where have we got to?

▌ For customers to engage, they need to find meaning in communities. These communities must be designed to allow for an exchange of ideas that leads to the co-creation of a product, a service or an experience. It is that act of co-creation that ensures meaning and therefore engagement.

▌ The 'formal' organization most leaders work with and aim to tame cannot cope with the needs of customers. In so far as it relies on rules, roles and economic incentives, it cannot cope with the desire of self-actualizing customers.

▌ The only way to build a community that can respond to customer needs is to establish connections across the organization that will enable every part of the value chain to co-create with the customer. These networks already exist in the organization. They are established by people as part of the normal rules of relating. The role of the leader is to capitalize on this 'real' organization to ensure that its energy is channelled towards the delivery of the organization's objective.

So, where do we go next?

Our view of what good leadership is about will determine the kind of leaders we are. For most leaders brought up in the 'formal' organization, good leadership is about getting people to follow. Whilst this may be sufficient in order to get people to fulfil their accountabilities, in the people economy it will never lead to success. Great people economy leaders are connected leaders. They make sure that they build connections across the organization capitalizing on 'real' networks. This requires them to change their view on leadership and the tools at a leader's disposal. In the next two chapters I want to introduce you to Gary (the CEO of a market leading company) and Dave (an executive in a consumer goods company). Together, they will show you how you can get your customers to follow by changing the 'what' and the 'how' of leadership.

3

What must leaders do?

Gary is no Samantha, Michael or Torsten. For a start he is happily married and, although he happens to be on a golf course every day, the only thing he drives on it is his car (his office is in the middle of a golf course). Unlike the others, Gary leads a real business.

Gary Lubner is the CEO of BELRON, the global leader in vehicle glass replacement and repair. BELRON companies (AUTOGLASS®, CAR-GLASS® and others) replace or repair a motorist's windscreen every seven seconds, 24 hours a day, 365 days a year. BELRON is an impressive business by any standard. With over 12,000 staff operating across 28 countries on four continents, BELRON has posted 20 per cent compound annual profit growth over the last five years. So why, in an industry with so much growth potential and fairly low barriers to entry, can't BELRON's competitors reach such a scale? Its closest competitor is about a tenth of its size and operates across only two countries.

Gary will tell you that 'It would take any MBA class a couple of days to come up with our strategy of branded, mobile replacement billed via insurance companies rather than individuals (for easier sales penetration and streamlined business processes).' So what is the 'BELRON difference'? Could it be people – a company's greatest assets according to many leaders (a spurious claim even if they meant it, as people are not owned)?

This would be too simplistic. After all, BELRON shares the same pool of qualified employees as its competitors. Gary is clear about the answer. The difference is leadership. He and his team show how leaders can be successful in a world where people make choices.

The questions this chapter will answer

▌ What do leaders do?

▌ What impact do leaders create?

WHAT DO LEADERS DO?

With over 5 million web pages combining the words 'definition' and 'leadership', the question 'What is leadership?' is as reasonable to ask as it is difficult to answer. Yet, clearly, the creation of communities of value in the people economy will require strong leadership. So, if leadership is now a core competence (as it is Gary's) that will ensure the successful passage of an organization through the people economy storm, we had better have a definition for it that accounts for what is different.

'I am their leader; which way did they go?'

To complicate matters further, definitions of leadership do not all focus on the same thing. Some define leadership as a role (eg the leader is the person at the top of a structure), whilst others focus instead on leaders' behaviours (eg leaders inspire others). Some even define leadership by focusing on the actions of others (eg a leader is someone who is followed).

This last definition, whilst being the least practical (it is easier to develop one's role or oneself than to develop others in their role as followers), offers the greatest scope for the delivery of value in the people economy. If leaders are to engage customers by building communities that bring value to self-actualizing individuals, they have to create connections between people in the organization to maximize the co-creation value of the 'real'. Therefore, their primary focus must be on the impact they have not just on their immediate team but on the organization as a whole. The question asked of all leaders in the people economy is 'Why should I follow you?' and the answer will never be 'Because I say so.'

Advocating a focus on followers' needs should not however be mistaken for advocating a Machiavellian 'I am their leader; therefore I must follow them' principle where the leader's duty is to do whatever it takes to remain in power, regardless of principles, purpose and equity. This approach overlooks the quintessential nature of people economy communities. You only follow someone because of the resonance that person creates in you. When no such resonance is in place, resentment and mistrust ensue. Leadership in the people economy is leadership in the 'real'. Leadership in the 'real' is not just about the social dimension (ie the network); it must have a moral dimension too in order to succeed.

Building a people economy definition of leadership

In the people economy, leaders add value by helping customers self-actualize. To do so they need each part of the organization to be connected at the 'real' to ensure co-creation, yet they also must achieve the formal business objectives. They must therefore apply a multidimensional definition of leadership that focuses both on their own role and on the needs of their followers, thereby reflecting the needs of both the 'formal' and the 'real' organizations.

To answer the question of what leadership is in a way that is replicable and ensures a healthy pipeline of leaders, Gary needs a definition that goes beyond the mere slogan (eg leaders are followed) or is overly conceptual (eg leadership is transformational and management transactional). Here is the three-part answer I have come to rely on to explain what it is that Gary and his team have become experts at:

▌ Connected leaders take personal risks in the pursuit of a key goal.

▌ Connected leaders influence others towards their positive engagement with a goal.

▌ Connected leaders create the perception of challenge and support within another person.

The leader as risk taker

The first part of the definition states that the role of the leader is to *be prepared to exercise personal risk in the pursuit of a key goal.*

What all leadership definitions have in common is the need for leaders to be personally invested in the journey with their stakeholders. As Chuck Jones, the VP of Global Consumer Design at Whirlpool, says: 'As a leader, you have to pick a hill and be willing to die on it.'[1]

Leaders must learn to pick the right hill. Chuck Jones made this observation when recalling how he threatened to resign when Whirlpool was stalling on the Duet concept (a separate washer and dryer designed to be bought together) that his team had been working on.

The Duet was a nightmare to produce, a costly affair rejected by customers in focus groups. You can't blame the board for stalling. Yet Chuck fought. The Duet was produced. As ubiquitous in its category as the iPod in its, the Duet's amazing results show that Chuck knew how to pick the right fight.

This is particularly important in the people economy because letting go of the levers of 'formal' power is a courageous thing to do. Connected leaders need to be able to choose their hill outside their function. They must stand for something bigger than a set of accountabilities and be prepared to fight for that something. But a leader who picks the right hill doesn't have to climb it alone. In fact, the danger with a leader choosing all the hills is that they may, in time, pick one no one can climb. This is where the next part of the definition comes in.

The leader as influencer

The second part of the definition states that the role of the leader is to *influence another person towards positive engagement with a goal.*

This emphasis on positive engagement indicates the need for an emotional response to a task. To have someone engage with a goal is easy. Economic incentives can coerce people into doing something. In contrast, to achieve positive engagement is harder. It is this though that makes the delivery of results sustainable.

Psychologists talk about discretionary effort. Discretionary effort is the amount of extra effort we have available in addition to the effort necessary for the completion of a task. It is called discretionary effort because it is ours to allocate as we see fit. We all have examples of times when we went the extra mile and times when we did just what was needed. Discretionary effort is not just nice to have. The release of discretionary effort from employees can lead to a variance in organizational performance of up to 30 per cent. That's a potential extra 15 per cent added to the bottom line.[2] In the people economy, getting employees positively engaged so they release their discretionary effort is critical. Connections across organizations can only be fluid if employees are prepared to do whatever is required to ensure co-creation. They cannot be limited by their function or accountabilities.

The role of leaders is to ensure that the right people are engaged in the right way at the right time to release their discretionary effort. In order to know what 'right' means in a given context, leaders need to engage in relationships with the organization's employees. This means that they will have to ensure they have the right impact. Engaging with individuals to help them release their discretionary effort means that leaders need to focus on the next part of our definition.

The leader as supporter

The third and last part of the definition is that the role of the leader is to *create the perception of support and challenge within another person*. Let me explain why I include the word 'perception' here.

People's perception is their reality. Despite our best intentions, our actions often have unintended outcomes – who hasn't purchased what they believed to be a perfect present for a loved one only to discover that this had later been returned to the shop? Leaders must ensure that what others perceive is indeed what was intended. If employees are to release their discretionary effort they will do so if they are rewarded with further personal growth (after all, in the people economy employees and customers are alike, in that employees too look for self-actualization opportunities).

It's all about you

So, in the people economy, leadership is the ability to impact others' personal growth by bringing together the three parts of the definition to ensure employees release their discretionary effort for the sake of establishing connections. In short, leadership is about making others grow.

I was working with an executive of a global consumer goods business who had just started a new high-tech division in Silicon Valley. She had to start from scratch. She had an idea, some incubation funds and a small team of like-minded individuals. She could have done what most other successful, driven and highly intelligent business leaders do. She could have designed organization charts and processes. She could have written strategies and plans. That's not where she started, however. She started by discussing the joys of entrepreneurship with her colleagues. She asked me to meet with her and her team to discuss the excitement of innovation and working in the unknown.

These discussions were all about rather esoteric stuff – stuff that would have frightened the executives who had entrusted her with a significant budget and factory time in Asia to produce what was yet to be invented. So I was rather surprised when I asked her why she did this and her answer was so grounded in the reality of engagement. This is what she said:

> The reason this is important is that at the end of the day we're in this together. I can make choices and I can ask them to make choices. But I can't make their choices for them and expect them to give 100 per cent. That means that the only things that will keep us on track are the discussions and interactions we have. Our passion is what will make this thing work. We need to make sure we talk.

Here she was capturing points one, two and three of the definition – goal, set and match!

The leadership difference

What is clear is that, to be successful in the people economy, leaders need to understand that the levers of traditional leadership no longer apply. The need to create a different kind of community with a moral and social dimension rather than a purely economic one means that the elements that make for leadership success are different. The new leadership levers are all features of a more collegiate, voluntary and two-way relationship designed to ensure the emergence of a community customers are happy to belong to. Clearly where 'formal' leadership could use the levers of power afforded to it by a world of human 'doings', in a world of human beings these levers no longer apply (see Table 3.1).

Table 3.1   Contrasting formal and real leadership

'Formal' Leadership	'Real' Leadership
Vertical	Horizontal
Directives	Dialogue
Hierarchical	Communal
Constrained	Flexible
Accountability	Reciprocity
Robust	Fragile
History irrelevant	History matters
Control of resource	Creation of trust
One-way	Two-way

A people economy community can only emerge if leaders display a different form of leadership. To create such communities, leaders must change the nature of their impact. Where once they could rely on their position to enforce effort, only their impact will now ensure the release of discretionary effort.

WHAT IMPACT DO LEADERS CREATE?

So, let's get back to Gary and his team. What matters here is not just how to define leadership, but how to define what leaders do given the constraints imposed on them by the people economy.

When we move from a model of leadership that relies on 'formal' instruments for influence to one that derives influence from a 'real' set of conditions, we need to rethink how leaders go about their task. If, for example, we have the power to hold people accountable, we need to be good at providing clarity about expectations. We need to pay attention to the details of contracts and obligations. We need to have the ability to select and encourage talented subordinates. We need to have the ability to confront poor performance.

But when the people economy takes away the levers of resource ownership and task allocation, many of these traits become inappropriate. Now self-actualizing individuals have to _want_ to help you in order to release their discretionary effort (ie prioritize your goal over all the other demands made on them).

As the stories of Samantha, Michael and Torsten show, what makes people want to participate, even though they don't have to, is a combination of factors. Perhaps they like or owe you. Perhaps they trust your insights or agree with your ideas. Possibly, simply, they see that what you are arguing for is the 'right' thing to do.

Impact becomes the leadership agenda

The key for Gary and his team to build a growth culture through leadership is to focus on creating an impact such that people will release their discretionary effort to achieve corporate objectives. What Gary and his team have become experts at is creating the conditions that make them magnets for relationships. What they have understood is that to lead successfully in the people economy you cannot rely on your position alone; you have to make people want to follow your lead.

The 'real' is a place of relationships and connections. As such, Gary and his team cannot control it. What they must do is create and sustain an impact so that people will want to engage with them in these relationships. Only then can they be assured that they capture the discretionary effort of their staff and engage in co-creating meaning with them. This will create the connections necessary to ensure customer engagement. The sum total of these relationships represents the social capital of the organization. In effect, it builds a people economy community. Such leadership is viral as opposed to positional, as the impact of leaders is felt throughout the organization via connections as opposed to the edicts they send. This ensures involvement and the release of discretionary effort.

Defining impact

Effective people economy leaders possess a moral authority that enables them to build social obligation through relationships. That in turn establishes the connections necessary to people economy communities. Therefore, to create communities of value, connected leaders need a reserve of credibility. This underpins their ability to build effective connections. It is this credibility that I call impact. Think about it this way. With whom would you rather have a relationship – the dour pessimist or the engaging optimist? Towards whom do you naturally gravitate – the authoritative leader who paints a picture you can see yourself in or the micromanaging financial expert who sets goals to be met?

To answer this question, in 2005, two colleagues from the Hay Group (Nick Jerome and Donna Gent), led by Russell Hobby, the head of Hay Group Education, set out to study what differentiates the people at the centre of the 'real' (the hubs in the 'real' network) from the people who are poorly connected. There were 984 people who took part in the study.[3] The results of the study into impact can be narrowed down to five elements, which followers describe as the source of a leader's credibility.

What I have found working alongside Gary and his team is that they have managed to create an impact where these elements are felt by people around them. It is this that accounts for the BELRON leadership difference. This is why they are so influential. In this book so far, we have met people whom others choose to work with because their relationships are characterized by these attributes. Interactions are safe, worthwhile, enjoyable, useful and straightforward.

Table 3.2 A holistic picture of leadership impact

Elements of Credibility	Why They Are Valued by Followers
Integrity	'I find them honest and transparent in their motivations and intentions.' 'The relationship is safe.'
Utility	'Our relationship is relevant to my concerns, and interactions are tightly focused on my goals.' 'The relationship is worthwhile.'
Warmth	'I enjoy our interactions and find them energizing.' 'The relationship is enjoyable.'
Reciprocity	'They are interested in my goals, as well as their own, and are genuinely helpful; there is something in this for us both.' 'The relationship is useful.'
Maintenance	'I don't have to work too hard to keep them on my side and they are interpersonally sensitive.' 'The relationship is straightforward.'

It is the impact they have on the business that has ensured Gary and his team lead an agile, focused and high-performance organization. They have managed to create an impact that enables them to lead the 'real' organization to achieve their 'formal' objectives. Let me illustrate impact using stories from BELRON.

Integrity

'I find them honest and transparent in their motivation and intentions.'

The first area of impact and the key to unlocking the discretionary effort of others is integrity. It is critical to be honest to be a leader in the 'real' organization. As the 'real' is a place of deep (rather than structural) relationships, only the whole person can be valued. No room is permitted for lack of authenticity. Integrity is achieved through the alignment of thoughts, words and deeds. A leader who preaches something but does something else does not score high on this dimension. Gary knows the impact of carrying thoughts to actions through words. In fact, he is fond of telling the story of his father Ronnie's interaction with a customer.

Ronnie Lubner led the business his father founded. Before the days of mobile replacement, customers had to drive their car to a local branch. One evening he received a call at home from a customer who had turned up to collect her car only to find her local branch shut. This being a Friday, she argued, she would be without a car for the whole weekend. Having found Ronnie's number she was phoning as much to vent her anger as to find a solution.

It took Ronnie less than two seconds to come up with a solution. His wife would drive her car to the local branch whilst he would drive his. The customer could have his car for the weekend and his wife would drive him back home. As a child, sitting at the dinner table, listening in on his dad's conversation, Gary couldn't fail to understand what customer service standards meant. Declaring that customers are important is one thing, but when the CEO gives you his car you know he means it.

Integrity in BELRON is critical. Standards are clear and adhered to. Failure to adhere to them is seldom forgiven. In a community, it is important to ensure that the norms that hold it together are strong.

Utility

'Our relationship is relevant to my concerns, and interactions are tightly focused on my goals.'

Out of all the components of impact, utility is the one that 'formal' leaders will recognize and indeed value as a key influencer of followership. Indeed, the very notion of economic incentives and hierarchies is built on the view that followers find utility in their contractual relationship with the organization ('They work because I pay them and that enables them to live the life they want'). However, in the people economy, where self-actualization is not just a secondary concern but the driver of engagement, utility is quantified differently. The notion of utility forms part of a dialogue the leader has with others to align the goals of the organization to those of its stakeholders. The interaction is rated against utility rather than just its outcomes. In that way, utility is not the same as necessity; it is the coming together of organizational goals and personal aims.

I have been lucky enough to talk to every senior leader in BELRON as well as meet with many of the top 200 leadership cadre. One thing they will all tell you is that BELRON is *their* business. They all feel as though they are in full control of events. Some will tell you that Gary gave them the business to run. Others will tell you that what happens is directly related to what they do, thereby recalling the need for co-creation explored in Chapter 1. By concentrating on the 'what', Gary has given people full ownership of the 'how', thereby enabling people to inject their personal passion in their work.

This area of impact has been largely ignored in recent years as most leadership development efforts have focused on behaviours to the detriment of skills and knowledge. Whilst this has been done for good reason (behaviours, unlike skills and knowledge, do differentiate for performance), it has been forgotten that skills and knowledge are the prerequisite to effective leadership. To ensure that a relationship is worthwhile, leaders must be credible in both what they can do and what they know. Gary knows the business inside out. He is as credible when he talks about financing an IPO as he is when he explains how to replace a windscreen. Connected leaders do not have to know everything but they have to know enough to inspire confidence in others (by the way, the integrity dimensions ensure that being a good liar is not enough). They approach each relationship with the aim of answering one question: 'Have I made this individual feel stronger and more capable?' They can only answer yes if they have the skills and knowledge as well as the behaviours that engender 'utility'.

Warmth

'I enjoy our interactions and find them energizing.'

Following Gary when he is on one of his branch visits or indeed watching him interact with people will tell you all you need to know about how much he is liked by people around him. The energy in a room increases as he enters. Of course, much of the reason why people find interactions with Gary enjoyable is that he knows every area of the business and is clearly passionate about it.

Warmth, however, does not come from undifferentiated praise. Before being CEO, Gary used to head up the UK business. Then, like today, Gary would spend time on the road visiting branches and talking to staff. This proximity and his obvious love of the business are what make him such a popular visitor amongst branch managers throughout the world. But this brought with it a problem: Gary was too nice!

Gary enjoys meeting people and delights in others' achievements. He made a point of congratulating anyone he met who had achieved anything until, one day, he was told by a member of his team that his praise was starting to lose value. The problem was that the same praise was given regardless of the size of the achievement. Nowadays, Gary has not stopped being nice; he has just learnt the exchange rate of the 'recognition currency' in his business. He hasn't stopped delighting in the achievement of others though.

Connected leaders like Gary will always want to ensure that they are approachable. Gary recalls the time he walked into the office speaking on his mobile phone looking annoyed and uttering the words 'The sale must go through.' Rumours of an impending sale of the business started and Gary's apparent outrage did not lead others to ask him for details. If they had, they would have known that selling his second-hand car had been on his mind that morning, as his wife was discussing with him a potential problem with the sale.

Reciprocity

'They are interested in my goals, as well as their own, and are genuinely helpful; there is something in this for us both.'

One of the tenets of the people economy is reciprocity. As we saw in previous chapters, the communities of value human beings long to belong to are founded on the principles of reciprocal moral and social obligations. Just as valuable as Gary's ability to make relationships useful is his capability for building clarity without closing options.

Gary is clear: his business is about vehicle glass replacement and repair. Liking to think of myself as an innovative type, I suggested when I first met Gary that BELRON should apply his business model to tyres and exhausts. Gary's answer, 'That's not the business we are in', could at best have appeared to stifle innovation and at worst to kill my excitement. However, what Gary had done was articulate boundaries within which people's imagination enables them to excel. He spent time explaining the need for the boundary (investment is limited and growth can still be gained from optimizing the current business).

At the same time, Gary relies on dialogue to enable others to input their ideas and thoughts. In a global organization, it is hard to be certain of what will happen next. The challenges in each local market are different and the local cultures impact the business in many ways (when the French government instituted a crackdown on speeding, the French business saw sales fall as pebbles no longer hit windscreens at glass-breaking speed).

It is impossible for any leader, even one as versed in the business as Gary, to provide answers to all the questions. Reciprocity is the only way to ensure others contribute. Watching Gary operate in meetings, you quickly realize that building organizational clarity means being able to surface 'real' uncertainty. When Gary talks, he asks questions, a lot of questions. What is your biggest challenge? How is the market? What is going well? The aim of the questions is not to catch anyone out or even gain control over his business but simply to help put things in perspective. Gary is as much a 'clarity broker' as he is a leader. Someone somewhere in BELRON has the answer to someone else's problem. Gary's job is to put them in touch with each other.

Reciprocity ensures that the provision of clarity is not about uncovering some hidden truth, but rather about building a common frame of reference. This reliance on a shared sense of direction and identity builds reciprocity.

Maintenance

'I don't have to work too hard to keep them on my side and they are interpersonally sensitive.'

Maintenance is the oil in the relationship machine. A leader who scores high on all the other elements of impact can get away with making a relationship hard to maintain, but only for a limited time. Everyone has examples of leaders or organizations that have disregarded the interest of their stakeholders but are so incredible in what they do or offer such a unique product that the relationship continues. Such leaders however cannot survive such changes in context as the people economy, as no community has been built in which customers are invested. Similarly, the release of an employee's discretionary effort can only be ensured if the relationship is reciprocal. This is unlikely to happen when leaders see themselves as infallible. As the world changes, customers and employees will move on.

The elements of impact are important because they offer an insight into why customers might stay in a relationship with the organization. They will only do so if employees apply their discretionary effort to the building of connections across the organization, as this alone will ensure co-creation. Hard-to-maintain relationships can release effort, but are unlikely to release discretionary effort. Even a relationship that is relevant, two-way and energizing will not survive in the long run if it is too hard to maintain.

Of course, maintenance is part of the BELRON DNA. The business is based on the idea of low maintenance. A windscreen fitter will come to you. In most markets, your insurance company rather than you will be billed for the repair or replacement. The service and branding consistency ensures that customers know what to expect. But maintenance is not only displayed in what the company does; it is also an integral part of the way people work. Low-maintenance relationships ensure that people release their discretionary effort.

On a wet morning in a hotel car park I was standing by my car talking to a fitter repairing my windscreen. I had been in a meeting with some of BELRON's senior executives and I jokingly proposed to test the service by calling the BELRON call centre to get someone to come and repair a crack in my windscreen. They had taken me at my word. As it was cold and wet, the only thing left for me to do was to understand a bit more about BELRON. The fitter who came was a young man clearly surprised to meet a customer so interested in the ins and out of repairs (I wanted to judge how engaged people at the front line were). It was clear that he was passionate about the technology underpinning his work. He talked at length about how the resin gets injected into the glass and the hardening process that makes it unbreakable.

As we were talking, Gary arrived at the hotel for the second half of the meeting. Upon seeing the fitter he started to engage in the discussion. He told the fitter how one of his first jobs at BELRON was to find a machine that would inject the resin. They discussed workarounds and health and safety issues. Gary retold the story of a fitter who was annoyed by the new uniform some years before and how he ended up getting him to lead a team of fitters to work with a designer to redesign the uniform. They discussed how they could help customers understand better the ease of repairs and the necessity to get repairs done quickly to stop impurities settling in the crack. After the repair had been completed and Gary had gone in, the fitter turned around to me and said: 'That guy is great, isn't he? It's great to see some of our senior people interested in what we do.'

Many leaders interact with people. Many do so in an engaging way. But few manage to isolate themselves from the CEO disease – the higher you go in an organization, the less you hear what truly goes on. In Britain, they say that the Queen thinks the country smells of fresh paint, as every building she visits has been freshly repainted. What Gary's story illustrates is that he had engaged with the fitter beyond the 'formal' boundaries. By the time he left, the fitter knew he had had a valuable discussion with a senior executive. Gary did not have to rely on his position. To this day I am not sure the fitter realized he had spoken to the CEO. What mattered was simply that he left with the feeling that Gary was 'an easy guy to get along with'. Of course, most leaders will set out to have an impact on the people around them and most leaders will set out to release the discretionary effort of their stakeholders.

The source of impact

Again, it is important to stress the proposition that was made at the start of this chapter. For a leader, it is not your intent that matters but the perception of the people on the receiving end of your impact. It is others' perception of the leader's impact that creates value. What ensures that Gary and other people economy leaders have a positive impact that releases discretionary effort is their beliefs about leadership. Connected leaders have in common a different set of beliefs about where their leadership impact comes from. That is why, in the next chapter, I want to introduce you to Dave, a leader who has mastered the art of people economy leadership and has delivered the results to prove it.

THE 30-SECOND RECAP

There are a number of definitions of leadership. Whilst some focus on the job and others on its incumbent, the best define leadership on the basis of what followers do. To be useful, a definition of leadership in the people economy must focus not only on what a leader does but also on the impact the leader has on others. The following is the definition of leadership at the 'real'. Leadership is:

▌ being prepared to exercise personal risk in the pursuit of a key goal;

▌ influencing another person towards positive engagement with a goal;

▌ creating the perception of support and challenge within another person.

The role of connected leaders is to ensure that there are sufficient connections in the organization to ensure that a community of value is created. They do so by having an impact beyond their immediate teams. In practice, leaders have an impact that will either help or hinder their positioning inside the 'real' organization. To become leaders based on their moral rather than their positional authority, leaders must have an impact that makes others want to be led by them. The nature of that leadership impact is best defined by looking at five dimensions of impact (see Table 3.3).

These areas of impact create communities. To have the right impact, a leader needs to understand what lies at the root of the impact that turns a 'formal' leader into a magnet for 'real' relationships (ie a connected leader). This is where Chapter 4 takes us.

Table 3.3 A holistic picture of leadership impact

Elements of Credibility	Why They Are Valued by Followers
Integrity	'I find them honest and transparent in their motivations and intentions.' 'The relationship is safe.'
Utility	'Our relationship is relevant to my concerns, and interactions are tightly focused on my goals.' 'The relationship is worthwhile.'
Warmth	'I enjoy our interactions and find them energizing.' 'The relationship is enjoyable.'
Reciprocity	'They are interested in my goals, as well as their own, and are genuinely helpful; there is something in this for us both.' 'The relationship is useful.'
Maintenance	'I don't have to work too hard to keep them on my side and they are interpersonally sensitive.' 'The relationship is straightforward.'

THE LEADERSHIP TAKEAWAY

Here are the points from Chapter 3 that are pertinent to the way you think about leadership:

5. *Leadership is about being followed.*

   - To be successful, leaders need to focus on others' perceptions and needs.
   - They will therefore need not only the courage to stand firm for what they believe but also the willingness to support and challenge others in their search for meaning.

6. *Your impact as a leader dictates organizational outcomes.*

   - Leaders have a direct impact on the way it feels to work alongside them. This impact encourages or inhibits the release of discretionary effort.

- The leadership agenda is therefore to create an impact that releases discretionary effort by ensuring that individuals' desire for relationships that are honest, useful, warm, reciprocal and easy to maintain is matched by the reality. The impact dimensions are the critical influencer to the release of employees' discretionary effort in the people economy where a leader's focus needs to be on creating enough 'real' connections to ensure the organization becomes a community of value for customers looking to self-actualize through co-creation.

4

How can leaders succeed?

Like Gary, Dave is a real leader. Like Gary, Dave is a high-performing leader. Like Gary, Dave creates an impact that makes others want to follow him. The reason I want to introduce Dave to you is that, the first time I met him, he told me his story. That story is the story of how to lead in the 'real' to engage the performance of an entire community.

Dave is pretty much the antithesis of a 'new age', fad-obsessed leader. In fact, coming from the town of Liverpool in the north of England and built like a rugby player, straight-talker Dave could not be any more grounded in reality if he tried. When you add to that the fact that, when I first met him, he led a soap powder plant, attached to a margarine plant, in the heart of the Czech Republic, you quickly understand that little is as gritty and real as what he does!

Dave Neil is a senior executive for Unilever in the Czech Republic. At the height of Unilever's Path to Growth strategy, his brief was clear: 'We will look at the revenue side of the equation. Your job is to minimize costs.' His story reinforces everything this book has been about so far. Engagement through self-actualization, communities of value and the 'real' organization are all concepts that dictate the way he works.

Dave's story illustrates how achieving high performance is changing. Here is what he did and what it can teach us about what leaders must do.

The questions this chapter will answer

▌ How do leaders achieve high performance in the people economy?

▌ What is different about the new high-performing leaders?

HOW DO LEADERS ACHIEVE HIGH PERFORMANCE IN THE PEOPLE ECONOMY?

The previous chapter's definition of leadership stated the need for leaders to take personal risks. Personal risk is something Dave knows all about. On a cold Sunday, he took his suitcase, left home and boarded a plane for Prague. Despite the fact that he did not speak a word of Czech, Dave was about to have conversations that would change his life as well as those of many others.

The challenge

Dave's challenge was an all-too-common business challenge. Unilever had promised their investors growth figures, which were not forthcoming. The top team had decided on a courageous Path to Growth strategy. They were about to undertake one of the boldest transformations in the consumer sector for some time. They would cut the number of brands from 1,600 to 400. They would centralize some investment and build synergies. The all-powerful regions would become the sales channel for powerful central branding. New processes would be created. The 'formal' organization was about to be disrupted. The 'new formal' was being formed.

In this context, it was paramount to get costs under control. The long-term latitude investors would give Unilever for revenue growth had to be paid for by short-term cost savings. The Path to Growth strategy, its history and eventual downfall are well documented. Dave though has yet to make the headlines: nevertheless, he managed consistently to deliver results that exceeded expectations in the midst of the Path to Growth storm (during which expectations ran at an all-time high).

The 'what' and the 'how'

Chapter 3 showed us that, for employees to release their discretionary effort and ensure the connections necessary for co-creation, leaders need to have a certain kind of impact. The way leaders create that impact given the constraints placed on them by the people economy is critical to the performance outcome.

To achieve results, Dave needed to get his team to align quickly to the corporate needs. Many leaders in his position would have started with edicts, job descriptions, inspections, coercion and special incentives. The instruments of the 'formal' organization (roles, rules and economic incentives) do deliver short-term clarity of expectations and desired standards of delivery well. So imagine the shock experienced by Dave's managers when he did something different.

The dialogue (part 1)

Within his first week, having assessed the situation, looked at the key business metrics, understood some of the business fundamentals and formed some hypotheses, Dave brought together his three key managers for a meeting. As he walked into the room with a pile of papers under his arm, the managers must have been waiting for the instructions they thought they were about to receive. This is what happened.

Sitting down at the table, Dave started to talk about Liverpool. He described the docks and his childhood playing in the streets. He talked about the Beatles and Liverpool's famous football club. He recalled how, at the same time as the labour movement was darkening the future of the Czech Republic, it was providing hope to the workers of Liverpool. He shared his passion for his job and his values around fairness and equity.

He asked them about their country. He wanted to know everything. They described the harsh realities of the communist era but also the simple pleasures they had now lost. They talked about the community that had come to rely on the plant. They talked about their dreams and their expectations. They talked about their children. Dave's natural curiosity was infectious. The discussion went on for hours. Soon, Dave started to call them the three musketeers, as they all talked at the same time about the same things ('one for all and all for one')!

Formal versus moral influence

The people economy requires leaders to reconnect with the full humanity of people. They must do this by creating communities of value in which people can self-actualize. The difference between communities of value and hierarchical communities is that the former rely on a combination of moral and social obligations as well as economic incentives to flourish. This can only be sustained through 'real' (ie moral) connections rather than 'formal' (ie positional) mechanisms.

By exploring issues such as identity, expectations and meaning, rather than relying on his positional power as a main source of influence, Dave created a moral connection between himself and his managers. Together they forged a moral bond and a shared identity by discussing their dreams and challenges.

In this way, Dave established himself as what many call an authentic leader. By sharing his story as well as exploring theirs, Dave highlighted to his managers that his thoughts, words and deeds were indeed aligned, thus creating the resonance necessary for 'followership'. He built integrity and warmth in the relationship and started to establish a sense of reciprocity.

The nature of leadership impact

Of course, whilst the moral source of Dave's power allowed him to start building a community of interest and consequently releasing discretionary effort, on its own this would have done little to ensure the co-creation needed to produce a valuable output for the organization. In effect, so far, the dialogue described gave Dave the right to challenge and support his managers in a way that built commitment.

Deriving power from moral authority does not ensure results until that power has been exercised. Influence without impact is of little use. A leader's impact must result in a relationship that is productive. In effect, this dialogue does not, in itself, channel engagement towards the achievement of a goal. What happened next did.

The dialogue (part 2)

Understanding people has always been important to Dave. He is a talker but also a great listener. When you speak to him, you feel that you are the only person in the world who matters. But Dave is also a businessman and wants to remain a successful one. He understands the importance of execution.

What he shared next with his team was his aspirations. He was, he said, going to make sure that, whatever happened, nothing ever came as a surprise. 'We will always be ready to face reality', he told them. 'This place is more than a plant. The village depends on us. We all depend on each other. So where do we go next? What do we need to do? What do you think?'

It was getting late but the conversation didn't stop. Dave had opened the gates that would allow the flood of ideas to come rushing into the meeting room. The last two areas of impact had been felt. Utility and maintenance were in place. Dave's impact was now likely to create positive engagement.

Social versus formal impact

If the first continuum for leaders in the people economy is about the source of their influence (ie from positional to moral), the second has to be the nature of their impact. As we saw in Chapter 3, in the people economy the impact of the leader cannot solely be economic (ie formal); it must also be social. A community, in the people economy, can only be of value if it is held together by a sense of shared responsibility for co-creation. To ensure that the 'real' organization functions in a focused, goal-oriented way, the impact of power matters as much as its source.

By opening the challenge to his team, Dave ensured the co-creation of solutions. By emphasizing the need for their experience, expertise and help, he ensured that he laid down the basis for social obligations. It is worth noting that Dave did not surrender leadership. Using a mixture of participation and vision, like Gary, he ensured that he was acting as a hub for the receipt and dissemination of meaning. By doing so, he distributed leadership across his team (and eventually they did too across their own teams) to maximize the positive engagement of all.

Dave's story continues

Dave's impact did not take long to yield results. As Unilever's Path to Growth strategy unfolded, pressure for results increased. Dave was asked to shut the factory to save costs further. Faced with an edict to implement, Dave called on the musketeers and carried on the discussion that had never really stopped since that first day. Even though the end was near for the factory and maybe the village, his position in the 'real' enabled him to continue connecting with his team in a way that his 'formal' position could no longer ensure (formally he was part of the leadership that threatened to close the plant).

Armed with their new-found confidence, a sense of shared meaning and maximum discretionary effort, Dave saw his team work harder than ever before. The discussions, which by now were not just confined to the leadership team but had become normal features of business in the plant, increasingly turned to purpose, meaning, organization versus individual agenda, and clarity. The team put together a plan not just to save the factory but to turn it into something bigger than it had ever been. They didn't look to survive; they wanted to thrive. Having laid out their plans on PowerPoint slides and Excel spreadsheets, Dave and his musketeers got on a plane to Brussels to a regional senior management team meeting they had not been invited to and convinced the assembled leaders to listen to them. Dave is now leading the transition that, far from shutting the plant down, will lead this to become a production hub in Europe.

WHAT IS DIFFERENT ABOUT THE NEW HIGH-PERFORMING LEADERSHIP RECIPE?

Maybe, in Dave's position, most of us would have started our new role by trying to get to know people better. What sets Dave apart is that, when he did exactly that, it was not a strategy to prepare his team for the 'formal' agenda that was to come – it was the only agenda. It was his way to think about leadership.

Making sense of 'formal' and 'real' leadership

Where others see hierarchies, the new leaders see connections. Like Dave, they have learnt to become critical hubs in a network of relationships. The headline difference between connected leaders and others is the way in which they, like Dave, impact and influence the world around them. Our role models and images of leadership are rooted in pre-people economy, hierarchical frameworks.

Consider this. As part of the interviews conducted for the research that underpins the findings in this book, Donna and Nick (mentioned in Chapter 3) asked each of the leaders with a higher-than-average number of connections to describe their view of leadership. The question we asked them was: 'What are the characteristics of a high-performance leader?' Table 4.1 lists the answers given by more than 75 per cent of one group

Table 4.1 Contrasting connected leaders' and others' beliefs as to what makes for a great leader

Highly Connected Leaders	Others
Innovative or risk takers	Diplomatic or tactful
Approachable or warm	Managerial or efficient
Communicator or listener	Knowledgeable or expert
Flexible	Credible

and less than 50 per cent of the other (ie the strongest characteristics reported by each group).

In essence, each group had a different picture of good leadership. It is these perceptions that shape our behaviours. These beliefs, values and behaviours go to create the nature of our impact, which predicts our success as leaders to a greater extent than even our skills.

The source of impact

Impact is the result of a number of factors. An iceberg is often used to describe these factors. At the top of the iceberg, there for all to see are skills and knowledge. As mentioned in Chapter 3, skills and knowledge are important because they give a leader the ability to take part in the game. On their own, they do not differentiate between average and superior performance. But to dismiss them, as many have done, as mere requirements is to miss their importance. Indeed there cannot be superior performance without performance.

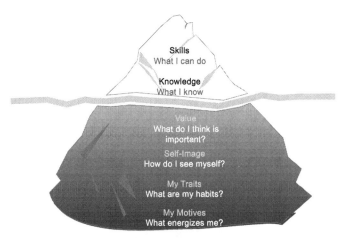

Figure 4.1 The iceberg model of sources of impact

But it is below the waterline that the real differentiators lie. In the murky waters below the waterline, the drivers of impact can be found. Performance will differ depending on how people see their role. If doctors believe that their primary role is solving problems, their behaviour is likely to be different from that of surgeons who see their role as healers. To be effective in leading at the 'real', leaders must build a new set of beliefs. Here is how these beliefs differ.

The areas of impact

The main differences between leadership beliefs reside in the way we understand our ability to impact and influence as leaders. In essence, this is about our understanding of the nature of power. What is clear is that leaders all have, and exert, power in one form or another. Dave's story, along with Donna's and Nick's research, shows how leaders gain and use their power differently. Connected leaders (ie the leaders who maintain a large number of relationships at the 'real') gain their power from their authenticity (the moral dimension) and distribute it to enable others to grow (ie the social dimension). Figure 4.2 shows the configuration of these different power-inputs and power-outputs.

Combining these dimensions not only shows how connected leadership comes about, but it also offers a number of development entry points depending on where a leader sits at any one point in any one context. Each of these quadrants is underpinned by a set of beliefs on what leadership is about. It is these beliefs that we need to address to have a new impact.

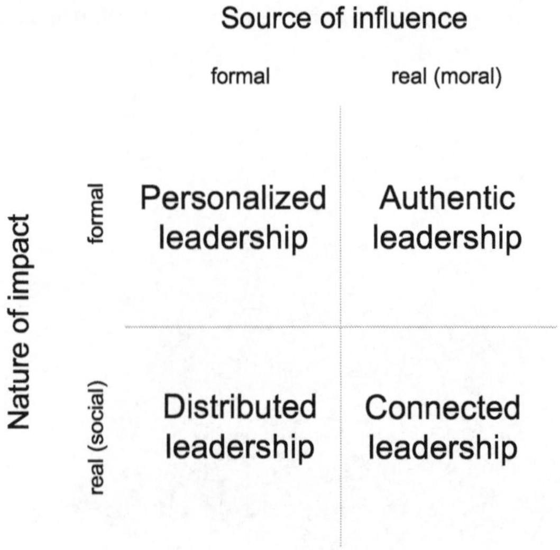

Source of influence

	formal	real (moral)
formal	Personalized leadership	Authentic leadership
real (social)	Distributed leadership	Connected leadership

Nature of impact

Figure 4.2   Four models of leadership

Personalized leadership

Personalized leadership has become a caricature of leadership. Personalized leaders derive their power from their position (ie their place in the structure) and have a direct impact on output through the use of what I have called economic incentives (ie 'formal' instruments).

The model has been much decried as outmoded over recent years. Headlines that proclaim the death of the star CEO abound. Yet it is still one of the most prominent types of leadership found in organizations. Even without turning to the extremes that make the headlines, the beliefs and values of this most 'formal' form of leadership are as follows:

▌ *Leaders have power over people by virtue of their position.*

Whichever way it has been disguised, this fundamental premise underpins many of the beliefs of personalized leaders. They embody and act the role, regardless of any personal characteristics. The position rather than the person holds power, yet the person who holds the position expects that power.

▌ *The job of the leader is to get others to conduct tasks.*

The job of the leader in a personalized mindset is not so much to create followers as to create doers. The people fulfilling an economic role (customers or employees) can be replaced should they fail to understand the nature of the relationship (or contribute below the optimal price point for the task).

▌ *People who do not willingly engage are not motivated.*

Critical to the success of personalized leadership is the necessity to place the responsibility for motivation on others. Rather than see lack of motivation in an employee as a failure to influence on the part of the leader, personalized leaders expect 'self-motivated' employees.

▌ *The leader is in charge of strategy and plans.*

In this quadrant, emphasis is placed on the ability of the leader to dictate the future and remove disruption from plans. The very essence of the 'formal' instruments that create personalized leadership is control and fear of deviation.

▌ *People work for an income and can therefore never be fully invested in a relationship with the organization.*

This is a long way to express a simple premise: people cheat. The belief is that people are not motivated by anything other than economic incentives and as such have no moral or social obligation to the organization. This, unfortunately, is not so much a belief as a self-fulfilling prophecy. As we saw in Chapter 2, wanting plus doing will always equal cheating.

As personalized leaders' skills lie in their ability to plan the future and keep disruptions to a minimum, this quadrant relies heavily on IQ and personal drive in order to get results. Even assuming that a leader can be savvy enough to see all the potential obstacles standing in the way of an organization, unfortunately IQ is not a differentiator of performance; most leaders have a similar IQ. Likewise, an unmanaged drive to achieve leads to unwanted behaviours displayed purely for the sake of winning (ie winning whatever the cost).

Distributed leadership

Realizing the limitations of the 'leader is omnipotent' model used in personalized leadership, distributed leaders recognize the power of others' input to the strategy and plans. Whilst in practice this type of leadership looks a lot more collaborative, it is still anchored in a set of beliefs that make it very much personalized (at least in terms of source of power). These beliefs can be articulated as follows:

▌ *Leaders have power over people by virtue of their position.*

Distributed leadership focuses on the impact of power rather than its source. In that sense it is the same as personalized leadership.

▌ *The job of the leader is to collaborate with others to get buy-in for task completion.*

Role holders are perceived as free agents who need influencing. However, this view still limits human involvement to the completion of a task rather than the co-creation of meaning.

▌ _People who do not willingly engage are missing on opportunities._

Rather than viewing people as lazy or cheats, distributed leadership views individuals as either engaged or not. For the distributed leader, resources are either contributory or not. The difference between both lies only in people's ability to recognize what is good for them.

▌ _The leader has ultimate decision-making power over the strategy and plans, albeit with collaboration and input from people at the design stage._

Whilst collaboration is encouraged, as with personalized leadership the leader remains in control of the interaction. The strategic choices followed by the organization are those determined by the leader.

▌ _People work for an income but can have a more fulfilling relationship if engaged._

In the same way as personalized leaders find it hard to understand their impact on the motivation of others, distributed leaders do not recognize that the source of motivation lies in the relationship rather than the transaction.

Here again, leadership is about IQ and drive but also requires softer engagement skills. In practice, this is a hard act for leaders to sustain as it lacks the authenticity necessary to create long-term engagement. Authenticity gives a moral tone to a relationship that ensures the building of trust. Without that trust, distributed leaders find it hard to gain the legitimacy necessary for sustained involvement.

Authentic leadership

More apparent in recent years, authentic leadership became paramount the day _Fast Company_ magazine announced that 'work is personal'. At the turn of this century, it was clear that, irrespective of economic conditions, the best people would always have a choice – to follow or to obstruct. It was also clear that the business world was not as transparent as some imagined.

As a result, the leader as a moral compass or, at least, the leader who derives power from his or her moral make-up has become a source of great interest. However, whilst some of the beliefs these leaders have about the source of their power are different, their beliefs about the impact of leadership remain constant:

▌ *Leaders have power over people by virtue of who they are.*

The shift from leadership being a role to leadership residing in an individual's moral make-up requires that leaders recognize that power (ie the ability to impact and influence) does not automatically come with the job title. They must pay attention to their relationships with others.

▌ *The job of a leader is to create the conditions for 'followership'.*

The first belief means that, when it comes to their role, authentic leaders see the need to influence. However, that influence is limited to the alignment of individuals to a plan rather than the co-creation of engagement.

▌ *People who do not willingly engage are limiting their choices, and leaders must highlight this.*

One of the issues with both distributed and authentic leadership is a paternalistic outlook. Leadership paternalism is an issue in so far as it limits the process of co-creation by not recognizing the equal value of contributions. It, therefore, hinders the release of discretionary effort in the people economy.

▌ *The leader is in charge of strategy and plans.*

Whilst the source of power has changed, its impact is still the same. Leaders, it seems, find it hard to let go of 'formal' control over the future of their organizations. This is a major problem in an economy that cries out for co-creation.

▌ *Whilst people work for an income, a vision makes engagement easier.*

When leaders realize that their power does not come from the leadership role, they also realize that it is their impact that creates engagement. Authentic leaders pay particular attention therefore to visions that excite their people. Whilst this does not change the nature of their impact, the method of developing a shared vision makes this somewhat more sustainable than a purely personalized approach.

Unlike any of the models above, connected leaders rely on a new set of beliefs that ensure the full potential of each individual is realized. The 'real' rather than the 'formal' organization becomes the main source of legitimacy and the main focus of effectiveness.

The shift to connected leadership

As we noted in Chapter 3, leadership at the 'real' is different. To be successful, leaders must ensure that both the source and the impact of their power is rooted in the 'real'. Leadership in the 'real' has history (ie there is a level of trust created or undermined by previous encounters). Personal style matters (ie 'Do I enjoy working with this person, as well as derive some utility?'). These relationships are powerful but fragile, and prolonged abuse can destroy them. Today, in the people economy, leadership power is measured by the number and quality of such connections.

Leaders who display this new type of impact (like Gary and Dave) rely on a different set of beliefs about the nature of their power. It is these beliefs that are at play in the connected leadership quadrant. It is these beliefs that enable connected leaders to be effective outside the boundaries of their intact team.

A new set of beliefs

▌ *Leaders have no power over people but have opportunities afforded by their role to help people grow.*

Connected leaders understand that their role does not give them power. What it gives them is opportunities, information and insights. Whilst these may be different from the opportunities, information and insights available to others in the organization, connected leaders know that they are not necessarily more valuable. Coordinating the wealth of ideas in an organization to enable people to make choices is what sets connected leaders apart. If leadership is about making choices, then making the right choices can only be achieved in connection with others.

▌ *The job of the leader is to facilitate the co-creation and positioning of a unique purpose.*

It is the belief of connected leaders that their job is mainly about the co-creation and 'selling' of a purpose. In effect, they act as conveners of a dialogue and debate that is larger than they are. They are not visionary in the sense that they are creators and custodians of a vision but they are authoritative in their approach to setting the tone that enables dialogue. It is this process that creates the alignment of individual objectives with organizational needs.

▌ *People who do not willingly engage are expressing a choice that reflects the lack of flexibility in leadership styles.*

Everybody is motivated in so far as everybody has motives. The leader's role is to ensure that these motives are appealed to and channelled for the completion of a goal. Individuals can choose whether or not to engage, but it is the leader's role to create an impact that facilitates that engagement.

▌ *The leader is in charge of ensuring the right strategic choices are made.*

To say that a leader is not accountable for strategy would be equivalent to saying that the leader's role is not about leadership. However, to say that the leader is solely in charge of strategy is also fundamentally flawed (since making a personal strategic choice requires no leadership either). That the leader is in control of strategic outcomes is only brought about by the illusion of control provided by the very economic incentives that destroy agility. What connected leaders are accountable for is ensuring that the right strategic choice is made. That is to say that they view their role as maximizing the opportunities people, wherever they are in the organization, have to sense what is going on outside the walls of the business (ie make the internal boundaries permeable to external influences).

▌ *Regardless of why people work, the nature of their contribution is influenced by their understanding of the availability of personal fulfilment opportunities.*

People work for a variety of reasons and it is not actually a leader's responsibility to encourage one as opposed to another. However, irrespective of the nature of their motivation, people make choices in the way they work that tend to reflect their need for self-actualization. The role of the leader is to ensure that people understand the opportunities for self-actualization that can arise from an alignment between their personal objectives and the organization's.

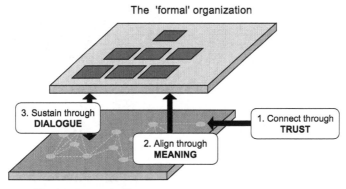

Figure 4.3   The levers of connected leadership

A new leadership recipe

Put together this set of beliefs and you get the very different kind of impact we saw Dave and Gary exhibit. What this enables leaders to do is pull on three levers to create the community customers crave by connecting their organization.

Trust and meaning are the currency of connected leadership, because people have to want to follow the leader. The reason connected leaders deal with this currency is that they understand the fact that people have options and make choices. Trust gives a leader the ability to let go of 'formal' controls, thereby ensuring that the connections in the organization are not disrupted by unwarranted 'formal' interventions. The co-creation of meaning ensures that the 'real' connections are targeted to the creation of a community of value that delivers 'formal' objectives. The release of discretionary effort can only come when the leader provides a compelling answer to the question 'Why should I do this?'

The main element of the 'real' organization, dialogue, makes connected leadership sustainable. Self-actualization occurs in processes of co-creation, which require strong dialogue. It is possible to make choices with no communication but it is difficult to make the right choices without consultation.

To watch Dave and Gary lead, you would be forgiven for thinking that some leaders are naturally predisposed to be connected leaders. Indeed, the way they both relate to others seems so natural as to be almost part of their genetic make-up. But the truth is different. Yes, both have a deep interest in others, but they also work hard at establishing connections. To pull each of these levers, Gary and Dave, like all connected leaders, have learnt to deploy new skills and behaviours. To show you how connected leadership can be developed, I want to explore their actions, their skills and their behaviours in the following chapters. We will start in Chapter 5 by focusing on the trust lever – why is it critical to achieving results in the people economy, how is it created and what leadership behaviours will sustain it? The humble banana plays an important role in this story.

THE 30-SECOND RECAP

A leader's impact is dictated by a number of inputs. At its roots lie a set of beliefs that direct a leader's actions. To be successful in the people economy, leaders must change their view of what power is.

Power is about influencing and creating an impact on others. Believing that this power comes from a hierarchical position will lead to behaviours that are counterproductive in the community-based people economy. At the same time, to assume that only the leader impacts the realization of goals ultimately leads to an over-reliance on economic incentives. As Table 4.2 shows, a lot of the traditional models of leadership rely on a similar set of beliefs.

Unlike leaders in traditional leadership models, connected leaders (ie leaders who create communities of meaning, thereby achieving higher performance in the people economy) rely on moral and social obligations to be effective. In practice, this means that they derive their power from a moral contract with others and impact the organization by distributing leadership in a way that creates social networks (ie creates a healthy 'real' organization).

The beliefs underpinning connected leadership are:

▌ Leaders have no power over people but opportunities afforded by their role to help people grow.

▌ The job of the leader is to facilitate the co-creation and positioning of a unique purpose.

▌ People who do not willingly engage are expressing a choice that reflects the lack of flexibility in leadership styles.

▌ The leader is in charge of ensuring the right strategic choices are made.

▌ Regardless of why people work, the nature of their contribution is influenced by their understanding of the availability of personal fulfilment opportunities.

Table 4.2 How traditional leadership beliefs evolve

	Leadership Beliefs		
Personalized Leadership ('formal' source of power 'formal' impact of power)	**Distributed Leadership** ('formal' source of power, 'real' social impact of power)	**Authentic Leadership** ('real' moral source of power, 'formal' impact of power)	
Leaders have power over people by virtue of their position.	Leaders have power over people by virtue of their position.	Leaders have power over people by virtue of who they are.	
The job of the leader is to get others to conduct tasks.	The job of the leader is to collaborate with others to get their buy-in for task completion.	The job of a leader is to create the conditions for 'followership'.	
People who do not willingly engage are not motivated.	People who do not willingly engage are missing opportunities.	People who do not willingly engage are limiting their choices and leaders must highlight this.	
The leader is in charge of strategy and plans.	The leader has ultimate decision-making power over the strategy and plans, albeit with collaboration and input from people at the design stage.	The leader is in charge of strategy and plans.	
People work for an income and can therefore never be fully invested in a relationship with the organization.	People work for an income but can have a more fulfilling relationship if engaged.	Whilst people work for an income, a vision makes engagement easier.	

THE LEADERSHIP TAKEAWAY

Here are the points from Chapter 4 that are pertinent to the way you think about leadership:

7. *Power is the great motivator.*

   - At the 'real' level, individuals need to be engaged through an effort of co-creation. This means that leaders must share the leadership agenda, which in turn requires an understanding of power.
   - Power, in leadership terms, is about influencing and creating an impact on others. Power in the 'real' rather than the 'formal' is derived from a moral make-up and used to create social networks.
   - Power is therefore given to the leader by others and has to be redistributed by the leader to make others grow. The leadership role is to be a hub in the middle of relationships, the purpose of which is the creation of shared meaning. This contrasts significantly with an image of a leader as creator of strategy, plans and staff alignment.

Diagnostic tools 2:

Are you ready to respond?

MEASURING LEADERSHIP IMPACT – THE IMPACT QUOTIENT

Understanding leaders' impact at the 'real' brings an understanding of how connected they are. This, in effect, gives us the level of social capital they create. The more connected a leader, the more likely the organization is to be agile. Impact is better judged by people on the receiving end of relationships.

Identify a person to whom you turn regularly for support. Evaluate the quality of that person's input to your relationship by completing the questionnaire below, thinking about your relationship with the person. There are 25 pairs of opposing words. Between them is a scale of five boxes. Consider your relationships with the other person: which side of each pair is most descriptive of the person's behaviour towards you (most of the time)? Do not take too long to complete this exercise. The way we relate to each other is underpinned by decisions we make quickly. Seldom do we even stop and think before we decide whether to associate with someone or not. Go with your instinct here. Mark the box that best captures the description (ie the closer to the word, the more apt it is). Thus, if you think the word on the left is highly appropriate, mark the first box. If you think it slightly or somewhat appropriate, mark the second. If you are entirely neutral between the two words, mark the middle box.

1. Honest						Dishonest
2. Transparent						Impenetrable
3. Consistent						Inconsistent
4. Reliable						Unreliable
5. Assertive						Submissive
6. Helpful						Frustrating
7. Purposeful						Aimless
8. Relevant						Irrelevant
9. Enlightening						Confusing
10. Beneficial						Detrimental
11. Fun						Grim
12. Optimistic						Cynical
13. Respectful						Manipulative
14. Amusing						Humourless
15. Energizing						Depressing
16. Pays attention						Inattentive
17. Can do						Jobsworth
18. Gives and takes						Takes only
19. Generous						Selfish
20. Modest						Domineering
21. Resilient						Fragile
22. Sensitive						Insensitive
23. Reasonable						Demanding
24. Independent						Needy
25. Relaxed						Suffocating

Having completed the questionnaire above, add up each of your results in the scoring template below. Moving from the left-hand-side box towards the right, give yourself a score of 2 for any answer in the left-hand-side box, then 1.5, 1, 0.5 and 0 as you move towards the right-hand-side box, as in the following example:

14. Amusing	2	1.5	1	0.5	0	Humourless

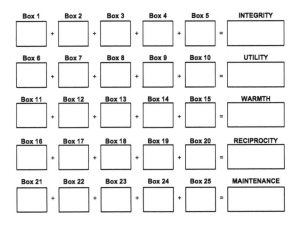

Now report each of your scores on the spider diagram below. This will give you the impact profile of the person you have just scored.

Integrity

10
9
8
7
6
5
4

Maintenance   3   Utility

2
1
0

Reciprocity   Warmth

Interpreting your results

The impact quotient should indicate the extent of your relationship with the person you have rated. The closer the person is to level 10 on any one dimension, the deeper and more sustainable your relationship with that person is. Missing even one element makes a relationship less sustainable. The definition for each of the dimensions is as follows:

Elements of Credibility	Why They Are Valued Credibility by Followers
Integrity	'I find them honest and transparent in their motivations and intentions.' 'The relationship is safe.'
Utility	'Our relationship is relevant to my concerns, and interactions are tightly focused on my goals.' 'The relationship is worthwhile.'
Warmth	'I enjoy our interactions and find them energizing.' 'The relationship is enjoyable.'
Reciprocity	'They are interested in my goals, as well as their own, and are genuinely helpful; there is something in this for us both.' 'The relationship is useful.'
Maintenance	'I don't have to work too hard to keep them on my side and they are interpersonally sensitive.' 'The relationship is straightforward.'

Using a red, amber and green system, it is easy to see how impact can lead to sustainable 'real' relationships:

▌ *Red.* If all dimensions score below 7, an individual does not create resonance. The person may still be in a leadership position but it is that person's formal rather than moral position that leads others to follow him or her. Whilst this is acceptable in a 'formal' setting, this individual will not be able to capture the value that resides in the 'real'. This person will not be able to create a community of value that customers would want to engage in to fulfil their need for meaning and growth.

▌ _Amber._ A relationship can be sustained for a short while at least if utility is in place – any individual can put up with a 'formal' leader if there are benefits in working with that person. However, over time, the high level of maintenance and the absence of other impact dimensions minimize the level of discretionary effort that people are willing to invest. Therefore, once again, the leader is not building any agility. If you find high levels of utility that are backed up by high levels of reciprocity (ie the person engaging in the relationship feels that his or her agenda matters) you have the foundation of a potential relationship. On their own, however, these two elements are not enough.

▌ _Green._ A balanced profile is one where all dimensions are at least above 7. This will ensure that a relationship can be built that is sustainable. Of course, the higher the number, the deeper the relationship and the more value can be gained at the 'real'. Without this, leaders will forever struggle to understand why they fail to respond to changes in context.

Next steps

▌ Having completed the exercise for a person whose input you value you may want to repeat it thinking about a person whose input you avoid. This will enable you to get a feel for the difference in impact of each group.

▌ Now we must turn to the hard task! Identify three people who you think respect your input and three people whom you would like to connect with better.

▌ Ask them to perform the same exercise, this time thinking of you.

This should illuminate your strengths and weaknesses as an informal influencer, identifying skills you can leverage and gaps to be addressed. It may help to explain why some relationships are working and others are not. The consensus of such perceptions across a whole team or an organization is one measure of the level of social capital within that group and of the richness of their connections and interactions. In effect, it enables leaders to understand how healthy their organization is. If we want to encourage a group to share information, learn from each other, support each other, act flexibly to plug gaps and communicate effectively, then social capital is a key asset. A process of self-evaluation like the one described above can identify collective barriers to creating this capital.

To ensure your impact changes, you will first need to examine your beliefs about what leaders have to do (ie your value set around leadership). The diagnostic exercise below can help you do this. Part 3 will help you understand the three key areas that, if developed, will help you increase your connected impact. Finally, Part 4 will help you build a development plan to further your connected status.

WHAT KIND OF LEADER ARE YOU?

As we have seen in the previous chapter, we all operate with a set of beliefs on what 'good' leadership looks like. The following questionnaire will help you reflect on the beliefs that underpin the way you view leadership. The instrument has been designed to outline the things that you value in leadership. This does not in itself tell us how your leadership is experienced by others (the previous exercise on leadership impact can be used as a surrogate for leadership performance in this instance).

Use the scale below to rate how important each item is to you when completing the statement 'Highly effective leaders...' There are no right or wrong answers – your opinion is all that matters. The rating scale is as follows:

4 = Extremely important
3 = Very important
2 = Important
1 = Of some importance
0 = Of little or no importance

Highly effective leaders...	Rating
1. engage others in making strategic choices through dialogue.	
2. make others grow.	
3. tell other people what needs to be done and how.	
4. get the most out of people by pointing out the opportunities available.	
5. check other people's work closely to ensure high standards are met.	
6. create the conditions that encourage others to follow.	
7. explain to people what needs to be done.	
8. explain to others the importance of doing work to a high standard.	
9. work with others to decide what needs to be done.	
10. understand the limitations of their own views.	
11. use others' insights to create a vision.	
12. secure others' input into their ideas.	
13. recruit an 'A' team of self-motivated individuals.	
14. work with others to release their engagement.	
15. understand how to get others engaged in the task.	
16. paint pictures for others that engage the whole person.	
17. train others to be able to deliver tasks to the highest standards.	
18. are able to shape the future by setting the best strategy.	
19. see selling the vision as a key leadership priority.	
20. highlight opportunities for others to grow.	

Having completed your rankings, transfer them to the template below:

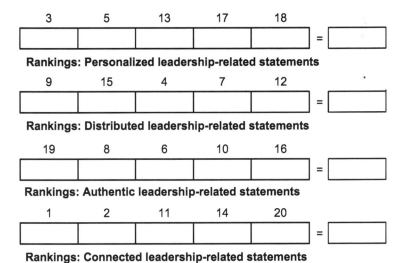

3	5	13	17	18	=

Rankings: Personalized leadership-related statements

9	15	4	7	12	=

Rankings: Distributed leadership-related statements

19	8	6	10	16	=

Rankings: Authentic leadership-related statements

1	2	11	14	20	=

Rankings: Connected leadership-related statements

Transfer these four total scores to the leadership-power profile. Do this by placing an 'x' at the respective total scores under the appropriate column.

Personalised	Distributed	Authentic	Connected

Interpreting your results

Each of the above statements carries some elements of truth in making leaders successful. However, prioritizing these on a scale of importance gives insight into the type of leadership that you are most likely to find of value.

Your behaviour as a leader is a function of both who you are (your beliefs, values, traits, etc) and the situation you are in (turnaround, established business, growth market, experienced or inexperienced colleagues, etc). There are no hard-and-fast rules governing the nature of the impact that you will have in any situation (ie your beliefs associated with a particular type of leadership might become more or less prominent in certain situations). It is clear, however, that your leadership line (ie the line obtained by linking the answer you have given on each leadership type) will indicate a profile of agility and resilience in the face of people economy changes. For example, if you have your highest scores on the personalized and distributed continuum you are unlikely to be building the moral authority sufficient to be an attractor (ie your impact, as recorded in the previous exercise, is likely to be low in particular on the warmth, reciprocity and maintenance dimensions).

Your impact as a connected leader will be higher, the higher your scores are in the two right-hand columns, as both authentic and connected leadership indicate that your impact is gained from your moral influence.

If all of your scores are below 10, it is likely that you are limiting your impact as a leader, as your beliefs are hesitant. In the people economy, it is better to have strong misguided beliefs than no beliefs at all, as long as one is open to challenge!

Next steps

You may want to get other people to complete this exercise, asking them to answer as they think you might have. This will give you insights into what their perceptions are of you (in relationships, other people's perceptions tend to be the reality).

There are three levers that connected leaders use to build resilience. These are trust, meaning and dialogue. These enable them to connect the 'real' layer of the organization to its 'formal' objectives in a sustainable way. It is important that you understand these levers, as they will influence your perception of what is valuable about the way a leader works. This is where Part 3 of the book takes us.

Part Three

The levers of connected leadership

Where are we?

▌ So, the role of a connected leader is to create an impact that releases the discretionary effort of employees.

▌ In turn, fully engaged employees use the 'real' organization to create the conditions necessary to co-creation.

▌ And all this matters because, in the people economy, co-creation through communities of value is at the root of customer engagement.

▌ The impact of connected leaders is driven by their beliefs about what great leadership is. It follows that, by changing their sets of beliefs, they can change the nature of their impact. Beliefs do influence outcomes. But how do we change beliefs?

Our beliefs are formed by our experiences as leaders. The influences we have had in our development have made us see some things as right and others as wrong. Beliefs are both influenced and reinforced by outcomes.

The easiest way to transform a leader into a connected leader is to change the actions that create impact. By getting results from new sets of actions, leaders will adjust their beliefs to reflect what works and what doesn't. To go from the bottom of the iceberg to impact is to translate a set of beliefs into actions that lead to impact.

As we saw at the end of Chapter 4, there are three levers of connected leadership. These are trust, meaning and dialogue. Each lever represents a group of actions that together deliver a connected impact:

▌ *Trust ensures integrity.* It enables leaders to connect with the 'real' layer, thus being able to start impacting the release of discretionary effort.

▌ *Meaning delivers utility and reciprocity.* It helps leaders align the organizational and personal needs, making sure that the release of discretionary effort is channelled towards the creation of connections.

▌ *Dialogue helps connected leaders create warmth and low maintenance.* It ensures that the alignment of 'real' connections with 'formal' objectives is maintained through constant reappraisal.

In the next three chapters, I will introduce you to a cast of characters who represent the spectrum of people economy actors from a supermarket shopper to a leader in a broadcasting corporation via a senior executive in an investment bank. All of their stories illustrate the actions connected leaders take that underpin a new way to lead in the people economy. Connected leadership can be developed. Here is how.

5

How to connect through trust

When Paul Wright came home on a June day in 2004 he did not expect to spend his evening in hospital. The cause of his hospital stay, being bitten by a tropical huntsman spider, is all the more surprising when you consider that home, for Paul, is Thanet in the very English and un-tropical county of Kent. Whilst huntsman spiders are not poisonous, they have a painful bite that can cause swelling, sickness and headaches.

The huntsman wasn't Paul's pet. It came from a bunch of bananas he had purchased at his local Tesco supermarket in nearby Broadstairs.[1] 'Biting the hand that feeds you' is a well-known expression but few of us expect to be bitten by our own food!

A week later, Tammy Neal, from similarly un-tropical Peterborough in the UK, became the second victim of the curse of the banana bunch. Her encounter with the spider was even more frightening than Paul's – around 20 small spiders ran across her arm as she was preparing to eat her banana. Even after disposing of most of the spiders, Mrs Neal could still not account for all of them. Worried for the well-being of her six-year-old daughter and three-year-old son, Tesco arranged for the fumigation of her house.[2]

Given that millions of bananas are sold by Tesco every day, the fact that these two events occurred only a week apart is bad luck. But, luckily for us, through their misfortune Paul and Tammy highlight the workings of the first lever of connected leadership: trust. Here is how.

The questions this chapter will answer

▌ Why is trust critical to connected leaders?

▌ How do connected leaders create and sustain trust?

WHY IS TRUST CRITICAL TO CONNECTED LEADERS?

Trust underpins an organization's ability to trade. For Tesco, this means having customers who trust that its products will not endanger their health. Customers may trust that an organization's product will always be of the best quality. They may also want to trust that the price is the lowest available. In fact, an organization has little control over the factors that lead customers to trust its products or services. The same applies to leaders – it is up to employees to give trust.

The sad truth about trust is that it can even be lost on the basis of others' actions. Yet, to be active in the 'real' organization, a leader needs to be trusted. Without trust, others will not want to engage in a relationship. 'Real' relationships are precious to employees. To have impact, a leader must have integrity. In the same way as trust is the foundation of an organization's ability to trade, it is the foundation of a leader's impact. It gives leaders their moral authority. So how do you earn or lose trust? Let's get back to the banana bunch.

The origins of trust

The UK is not a highly litigious society. Tesco was not taken to court over these incidents. Of course, the supermarket expressed concern, apologized for what was described as a very rare incident and made a gesture of good will (£200 and fumigation). But who was to blame? Who would you stop trusting (if anyone)?

Proximity says that you blame Tesco. Tesco, in turn, might blame its supplier. And, indeed, it did just that. Upon hearing the news of Mr Wright's spider, a Tesco's spokesperson declared 'We have been talking to our suppliers. . . We have obviously reminded them of the importance of ensuring that products are free of any foreign bodies, spiders in particular.' The supplier might be inclined to blame nature. After all, the fact that the huntsman managed to survive the sub-zero temperature it encountered on its flight from the Caribbean to the UK is a sure indication that it is a hard beast to eradicate.

In the complex web of relationships that makes up an economy, trust is distributed throughout the network. Someone else's actions can impact the trust we place in Tesco in just the same way as someone else's actions can impact the trust that is placed in us as leaders. Such is the power of networks. But where does trust come from? The key question an aspiring connected leader must answer is: 'What can I do to secure other people's trust?' A simple 'Be trustworthy' is the start of an answer, but things are rarely that simple. The allocation of an emotion (as trust is) is never that rational.

Rational trust

The good news, for leaders, is that human beings are wired for trust. Throughout the ages, the allocation or withholding of trust was critical to survival (ie 'Is this beast going to eat me or am I going to eat it?'). In the crowded and information-filled modern world, our need to make rapid choices requires the simplified wisdom afforded by trust. Human beings want and need to trust. Take the following experiment as an example.

In the late 1950s, Lefkowitz, Blake and Mouton from the University of Texas conducted research into what they called 'Status factors in pedestrian violation of traffic signals'.[3] To put it simply, they wanted to know 'Why did the man cross the road?' The experiment worked as follows. They asked a man dressed casually to stand at a pedestrian crossing and to cross the road whenever the 'Do Not Cross' sign was lit. When he did so, many looked on, but few followed. They then asked a man dressed with the 'attire of business and respectability' (until recently that would have been called a suit) to do the same. When he did so, many followed. In fact the suit increased the likelihood of people crossing the road by 350 per cent.

One can draw from this experiment the conclusion that trust, like many other things, is the result of rational judgements. People gather information on individuals (ie they know a business person who is trustworthy), test their hypothesis on a wider sample (ie the business people they encounter are trustworthy) and finally use this as the basis of a decision-making methodology (ie business people are trustworthy). If the situation changes (ie a few high-profile cases of untrustworthy leaders emerge), they review their opinion. On that basis alone, given the last few years, one may just want to try the experiment again!

The notion of rational trust does indeed seem to work. We trust certain professions over others. We trust people who work for organizations we trust. Leaders may trust people with specific educational backgrounds. We trust that, the bigger the brand, the more it is exposed and therefore the more likely it is that leaders will want to maintain its integrity.

Emotional trust

Our experiences form the benchmarks against which we gauge trustworthiness. All this seems logical enough. After all, all of us refine our judgement of what an individual can be trusted for as we gather more information. Often we will trust an employee to deliver against some tasks but not others (depending on our experience of the person's skills and similar projects). 'Logical trust allocation' satisfactorily explains both the impact of our deeds on our trustworthiness and the fact that others who belong to similar communities can impact that trustworthiness. As scientists and psychologists review their opinion of 'rational agent theories', however, new insights into trust are starting to prevail.

Embedded in the idea of 'logical trust allocation' is the premise that we differentiate emotional from rational responses. However, this separation of rational and emotional responses is coming under the spotlight. Psychologists have argued for some time not just that trust is the result of rational analysis but also that it comes from 'emotional' assessments. Scientists have now shown that human beings make trust decisions sometimes within the first minutes of an encounter.[4] We all have an emotional scanner, which works like the scanning device at a supermarket checkout. When we encounter someone we pass them through our emotional scanners to get a 'trust-no trust' response. The rational and the emotional are intertwined. We do not just remember our experiences rationally but, in fact, we allocate an emotional response to such rational assessments. The way our brains are wired means that we can recall an emotional assessment faster than we can conduct a rational analysis. In short, we don't think and then feel/react. We feel/react first and then we rationalize our behaviour on the basis of accumulated wisdom. We are emotional beings who react before we analyse. Trust allocation becomes an instinctive response based on accumulated emotional memories rather than just a rational decision-making process. So what does it mean in practice? We don't have to go back to the 1950s to see 'emotional trust' in action. In fact, let's fast-forward a couple of decades and consider the following experiment.

Rational + emotional = predictable trust

In 1968, sociologists Robert Rosenthal and Lenore Jacobson conducted a simple experiment. They administered a test to elementary school children to determine both their IQ and their potential for rapid progress. They identified two groups: 'unusually bright' children and 'average' children. They gave the class teacher the names of the children in each segment. At the end of the school year, the test was administered again. The children identified as bright showed, on average, an increase of more than 12 points on their IQ scores, compared to an increase of 8 points among the rest of the class. The teachers themselves could spot differences in behaviour and potential. They told researchers that the 'special' students were better behaved and more intellectually curious, showing greater potential than their counterparts.

Arguably, this was a predictable outcome. In the world of work, we know that high potential talent has a tendency to shine, or do we? What Rosenthal and Jacobson never told the teachers was that they had never actually ranked the children. They never took any of the original test results into account. They simply chose a random group of children, called them bright and let the teacher get to work. The Pygmalion effect was born. The teachers' expectations of their pupils made them behave differently towards each sub-group, creating an environment that encouraged the development of the 'brightest' group.

Through their very expectations, teachers have a direct influence over the performance of the children they teach. Like our teachers, we apply a Pygmalion effect to the way we allocate trust. Leaders have a direct influence over the health of the 'real' organization. The more they trust, the more trust develops. Of note for leaders is the fact that, unlike 'rational trust', which is adjusted on the basis of information, 'emotional trust' can be kept against evidence. Many politicians have survived the trust test despite well-documented evidence of their lack of integrity. Emotional trust provides a number of valuable insights for leaders. It shows how trust can be gained and kept even when making hard choices (which rationally others may not accept). It explains how a leader is at the mercy of others for the allocation of trust (hence the power of impact rather than just actions). But above all it does much more than that. It shows how trust can be made predictable.

Not unlike Tesco, which is at the mercy of its network, leaders too do not operate in a vacuum. The 'real' network is full of connections that can help and hinder trust. Using the Pygmalion effect, leaders can make trust a self-fulfilling prophecy by ensuring that 'real' communities develop a trust cycle. The accumulated emotional responses of the community ensure that, the healthier the 'real' organization, the more trust will be created. And, as with all good virtuous cycles, the more trust is present in an organization, the healthier the 'real' organization is. In a way, whilst the end does not always justify the means, the means invariably predict the end.

Connected leaders and trust

Connected leaders require people's trust to create or foster healthy 'real' communities. These communities help maximize social capital, thereby releasing discretionary effort. Trust forms the basis of the moral authority that allows leaders in the people economy to operate outside the counterproductive confines of their roles. Yet, as we have seen in the Tesco example, it is hard to see how trust can be sustained. Leaders, like organizations, make mistakes. While rational trust can be acquired through deeds, it would seem that emotional trust can only be created through consistency of actions and strength of impact.

Take the story of Chuck Jones and the Duet washer-dryer in Chapter 3 as an example of trust that could have gone wrong. After all, Chuck 'chose his hill' and created a revolution for Whirlpool by deciding to ignore the findings of customer research. But what if customers had been right? Chuck could have created a terrible product that no one wanted. Would we, as customers, trust an organization that constantly ignored our requests and opinions?

What helps organizations (Tesco) and leaders (Chuck) to survive the trust allocation decisions made by their employees is a concept akin to a 'trust account'. Imagine you have a 'bank' of credibility with your stakeholders, a reserve of trust that can be drawn upon to get messages across or influence the way things are done. Your behaviour (either rationally analysed or emotionally perceived) enables people to invest sufficient trust in you to allow for some expenditure.

The trust account

Chuck, because of his track record, skills and expertise, could afford to call in some of his trust-credits when faced with a tough call. Whilst surviving the curse of the huntsman probably made quite a dint in its trust wallet, Tesco had built sufficient trust-credits through its brand for its account not to go overdrawn when bananas attacked.

Engineering trust accounts is the way connected leaders ensure they earn the moral authority to lead at the 'real' just as effectively as they are able to lead at the 'formal' through their positional power. Observing how connected leaders relate to their stakeholders is like witnessing an old-fashioned view of relationships.

The actions of connected leaders exhibit two themes. Either they are concerned with the building of reserves, investing in and cultivating their bank of credibility and trust, or they are concerned with spending wisely. All leaders have trust accounts, whether they are connected or not. Connected leaders, however, are relentless in monitoring and managing their accounts. That is why, with connected leadership, history matters. The deeds of connected leaders must accumulate to form a trust account that is sufficient for them to assert their moral authority.

Working with the trust account

First, connected leaders take actions that may not deliver immediate personal benefits. This will build their reserves. Second, they are cautious about drawing upon these reserves unnecessarily. Savings are precious. Maintaining a rainy-day account enables leaders to take personal risks. Yet, as a result of their account management, connected leaders might appear cautious and conservative even when they are at the forefront of innovation.

There are a number of activities and behaviours that can be categorized in the 'investing' and 'spending wisely' categories. These ensure a connected leader is given permission by others to influence the 'real' in order to release discretionary effort. Connected leaders understand the power of trust that comes from their investment activities. Likewise, people's trust in connected leaders' power is sustained as a result of wise spending on the part of the leaders.

HOW DO CONNECTED LEADERS CREATE AND SUSTAIN TRUST?

As we saw in the previous chapter, Dave could have achieved short-term results by relying on 'formal' instruments, yet his behaviour as a leader (ie his ability to engage in dialogue) and his focus on the 'real' (ie relying on the co-creation of meaning) are what made him successful. The actions that connected leaders use to build trust are what differentiate them. So, what do connected leaders do and how do their behaviours contribute to the building of their trust account?

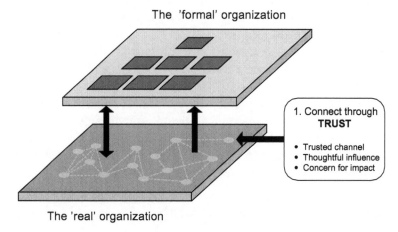

Figure 5.1 The leadership agenda, part 1

Figure 5.1 shows the three characteristics that underpin a connected leader's ability to build trust. These are the characteristics we will now look at in turn. The first step to becoming a trusted leader is to be a trusted channel.

BECOMING A TRUSTED CHANNEL

Connections are the lifeblood of the 'real' organization. Acquiring and sharing information is the way individuals construct the clarity that allows them to release their discretionary effort. This is best done when connections are plentiful and effective. In organizations, information flows are numerous and multidimensional (ie a lot of people talk about a lot of things and the same things can be talked about by a lot of people). To become hubs within that network (ie the only position that enables leaders to ensure the 'real' delivers the 'formal' objectives), connected leaders become valuable sources of insights and advice. They become brokers of information. They harness the wealth of data flowing through the network but give it some sense. They are the Google of the 'real'. They actively seek out information and pass it on to those who will find it useful. This is targeted networking, not blanket coverage. The latter would only increase information noise rather than give people insights for building clarity. Take the following example.

John's story

John works for a global electronics firm. When I first met him he had just been appointed to his dream role. He was in charge of working out the feasibility of a new product line. John had no reports (direct, dotted or otherwise). He had been given a green light to investigate the potential of an idea. Resources would be committed later if the first appraisal proved satisfactory. Yet John needed a lot of help. To understand the full impact of the potential line, he needed to gather engineering, marketing and sales resources. In short, he had a powerful mission with powerful potential, but no personal positional power.

John knew that to be effective he needed a team. He also knew that the easiest way to build a team when you have no positional power is to be the kind of person whom people want to follow. Integrity is right at the top of the list when a leader's impact is judged by potential followers. John knew that he needed a strategy to engage with others in dialogue to display his trust credentials. What better strategy than to make himself useful? John, as it turns out, made himself an indispensable hub in the 'real' network.

What John did

John became a broker of information. He walked around the organization and put people in touch with each other. He knew everything that was going on. Who was working on what? Who was thinking about what? He knew people's 'official' accountabilities and their 'unofficial' passions. He could unfailingly spot an opportunity to put two people together for their mutual benefit.

One day John organized a meeting with a vague title and invited over 100 people. As they gathered for the meeting he stood up at the front of the group, thanked them for coming and just told them that this meeting was about helping them. He then went on to introduce people to each other. Only minutes into the meeting, small groups formed. People were finally meeting like-minded individuals who could make their work easier – people who had answers to the questions they had. It wasn't long before everybody turned to John for advice. What John realized was that the 'real' organization chart is not made up of dotted or straight lines, but of a collection of information flows. In that network of information he had learnt how to place himself at the top of the hierarchy (ie at the centre of connections). Mapping the information network in his organization revealed that John was at the centre of most things.

Trusted channel and the trust account

By becoming an information hub, John exhibited all the hallmarks of connected leaders. He was building his trust account. By helping people connect, he was buying trust-credits. Colleagues all knew that they could rely on John for help (he always helped them even when they hadn't realized they needed something). This enabled John to get the help he needed. The 'real' power John wielded over the group was enormous, yet he never once had any 'formal' power over them. John could not command power, so instead he earned it.

The 'trusted channel' characteristic is the beginning of our model of connected leaders. It is the start of the journey to connected leadership. There are three things that are apparent in John's story and are consistent with the way connected leaders approach any issues:

▌ They position themselves in the flow of information – volunteering to take information from one group to another or to brief people after meetings.

▌ They work out what is useful for particular people to know – understanding other networks of influence.

▌ They take an active role in helping others to develop – securing external input when necessary.

The essence of this characteristic is taking consistent steps to become a vital conduit of helpful and focused information.

Actions that undermine trusted channels

The actions associated with becoming a trusted channel are in stark contrast to actions that are all too often seen in organizations where information is still seen as power. Connected leaders, unlike others, do not hoard information in the hope that it will give them a competitive advantage over others. That is not to say that they deluge others with information. John and others make an effort to understand who needs what and make useful connections. Connected leaders seldom copy and blind-copy others on e-mails for no other reason other than to cover themselves.

Connected leaders are trusted channels, not gossipmongers or trivia champions. Their use of information is authoritative rather than autocratic or automatic. In that way, they are able to exercise thoughtful influence.

EXERCISING THOUGHTFUL INFLUENCE

If trust and credibility are paramount for the connected leader, then the actions that undermine these should clearly be avoided, as trust account management requires the avoidance of unnecessary and unplanned spending. This means that connected leaders have to exercise their influence thoughtfully and cautiously.

Christine's story

Christine is an executive in a global beverage company. During one of our conversations, she recalled an unpleasant incident that had happened to her. Having conducted a strategic review of her business, Christine had decided to reposition one of the company's lines. One of her direct reports (a young executive hungry for success) had strongly disagreed with her during an executive meeting. Whilst the majority of her direct reports were in agreement that Christine's plan was viable and the young executive's concern had been largely addressed, it was clear to all that he would not easily be persuaded.

Christine had made time to walk him through the plans and bring him on board. After lengthy discussions, a way forward had been agreed by all. Not content with the outcome, however, the direct report went straight to Christine's boss to complain. He prepared a rationale and arranged a meeting. Let's just say that he was less than complimentary about Christine's proposed plan and questioned her ability to hold such a senior position.

After the meeting, Christine's boss called her and explained the situation and what he was about to do. 'I will sack him', he said. 'My reason is a simple one. In our organization, we just don't do this. If he is not mature enough to put his point across and accept the decision of the team, he should leave. I have scheduled a meeting with him next week to explain my decision.' What would you have done in Christine's shoes?

What Christine did

Whatever her feelings about this attempt to undermine her, Christine did not want to lose a talented executive. She also realized that her trust balance would suffer if she went along with her boss's wishes (surrendering this kind of decision to one's boss is never seen as a sign of strength never mind trust).

She called her direct report. I can only imagine what he must have felt upon being told that she wanted to speak to him. He must have known his time was up as he walked into Christine's office. What she said, however, was surprising:

> I know about your meeting with Mike and I know about your concerns with our strategy. I also know that you think I am about to make a big mistake. Having had positive feedback from many people and the whole team, I will stick to my decision. I do, however, need your help to carry this repositioning through and that is why I wanted us to meet. Mike did not look upon your request to meet with him kindly. In fact, he proposes to use next week's meeting with you as a way to remove you from our business unit and maybe even from the company. We have only one chance to get this right. So I would like us to spend the hour we have together to ensure that you come out of this meeting with Mike not only still employed as a senior leader here, but in a stronger position than you have ever been. After all, few of us get the chance to meet with a global executive leader twice in a matter of days! What do you think?

Talk about leadership being about making others feel stronger and more capable!

Thoughtful influence and the trust account

Christine's story shows that exercising thoughtful influence requires a high degree of self-control. Indeed, the absence of self-control is the single most important 'derailer' of executives' careers.[5] Unfortunately, our inability to control emotions is mainly down to the wiring of our brains. As I mentioned when talking about trust, neuroscientists now know that our primitive emotional brain commands actions before a complete analysis of all facts has reached the analytical brain. Connected leaders are not wired differently.

Like Christine, however, they are practised at keeping their cool in situations that would have many rushing into action. The four stages of connected leaders' thoughtful influence strategies can be summarized as follows:

▋ They plan and prepare their contributions carefully.

▋ They think about their impact on others and tailor their approach appropriately.

▋ They are empathic and sensitive to others' thoughts and feelings.

▋ They build alliances and connections in advance to support their case.

The essence of this characteristic is therefore the combination of two elements: planning in advance and sensitivity in action.

Actions that undermine thoughtful influence

Observing connected leaders does not yield any evidence of impulsive and extravagant gestures. At no stage are their interventions ill thought through or conducted for the purpose of self-glorification. The question at the forefront of connected leaders' minds is: for whose benefit am I doing this? Actions are taken only if the answer is: for the benefit of others (ie making others grow, as in the definition of leadership we have used thus far). As a result, exercising thoughtful influence means avoiding inflexible or verbose presentations and inarticulate or irrelevant contributions.

This does not mean that connected leaders avoid conflict. After all, like Chuck, to be successful they have to 'choose their hill and be willing to die on it' in order to be trusted. This is why the third characteristic of trust (ie having concern for impact) is so critical.

HAVING CONCERN FOR IMPACT

There is a seeming paradox inside the connected leader. Part of the reason they have so many useful connections is because they are credible. This matters to them. But another reason is that they get out there and forge connections, sometimes at the expense of both other people's and their own comfort. There is an inherent tension in being a connected leader. These leaders are motivated by the respect and trust of colleagues (by other people's opinion of them) yet they must occasionally create conflict.

Jane's story

On my third meeting with Jane I could tell something was bothering her. We had been talking for about 15 minutes, but Jane (a successful leader in a consumer goods company) didn't seem to be as engaged as she had been during our previous encounters. I asked her a couple of times if she was OK. Was she preoccupied by something? Did she need to reschedule our meeting?

Jane explained that she was not disengaged but distracted. She was deep in thought, as she was about to make a difficult call. In effect, she was reviewing her trust account statement before potentially going on a shopping spree.

Jane's problem

The reason Jane was preoccupied was because she was about to make a 'trust choice'. What transpired from our discussion was that Jane had an issue with another line of business in the company – one over which she had no power and with which she had few dealings. She knew, she said, that they were about to embark on a course of action that would lose the company money. This was not acceptable to her.

Jane is a connected leader, her network is vast, she operates out of moral authority in the 'real' and she knows how to create powerful social bonds around her. She had to make a choice: should she spend some trust-credit and potentially lose some personal credibility and goodwill or should she try to influence another way through her network?

The decision was hers to make and the outcome is irrelevant (I would love to say it all ended well but, actually, we never discussed that particular incident again). What matters is that Jane was demonstrating the behaviour that all connected leaders exhibit.

Having concern for impact and the trust account

Connected leaders show a deep concern for their impact. In effect, in managing their trust account, connected leaders are constantly balancing two imperatives:

1. taking actions that build the trust and respect of others; and

2. worrying about, and being sensitive to, their impact and reputation. The essence of this characteristic is a need to be respected and trusted rather than liked, combined with sensitivity to their reputation and impact.

Earning trust as a connected leader is not about courting popularity for its own sake. Often, the picture painted by stories such as John's, Christine's or Jane's is one of quiet leadership. But leadership cannot be serene and calm at all times. If connected leaders are to be successful in leading in the 'real', they have to demonstrate characteristics that reflect their humanity. People do not trust leaders who act the role. That means that connected leaders have to be themselves.

Actions that undermine having concern for impact

They do, however, need to show concern for the opinions of others. This does not mean shrinking from or avoiding conflict. This would be missing the opportunities offered at the 'real' layer. What's the point of having a surplus of trust-credits in your account and not spending them? Connected leaders do not need to be 'one of the gang'; they need to understand the gang.

The people economy makes trust easier to gain for connected leaders. Disconnection between organizations and people happened the day that self-actualizing human beings questioned the profit motive as the sole ultimate goal. When asked the question 'Which brand do you feel will be honest and fair?', UK residents put the post office as their most trusted.[6] People trust organizations that they perceive to have a higher purpose (in this case a service to the community).

In the people economy, providing meaning to people in search of identity is what establishes a connected leader's authority. Whilst people connect through trust, they can only engage through meaning. I never saw a better example of what I call engaging through meaning than Simon's story. I would like you to meet him in the next chapter.

THE 30-SECOND RECAP

For connected leaders to be effective in releasing the discretionary effort of others, they must be trusted. Integrity is at the root of effective relationship impact. Trust is the entry fee to a 'real' organization underpinned by reciprocity. However, trust cannot be demanded: to be of value, it needs to be given freely. People allocate trust in two ways. 'Rational trust' is allocated following an analysis of a leader's deeds over time. 'Emotional trust' is awarded to a leader on the basis of personal impact. Either way, connected leaders realize that they have a trust account to manage. They are obsessive about managing that account, saving credits or spending them wisely. To ensure that their behaviour earns a maximum of credit, they rely on three key characteristics.

First, they become a trusted channel. This means that:

▌ they position themselves in the flow of information – volunteering to take information from one group to another or to distribute and brief people after meetings;

▌ they work out what is useful for particular people to know – understanding other networks of influence;

▌ they take an active role in making people grow – securing training and securing external input when necessary.

The essence of this characteristic is taking consistent steps to become a vital conduit of helpful and focused information.

Second, they exert thoughtful influence. This means that:

▌ they plan and prepare their contributions carefully;

▌ they think about their impact on others and tailor their approach appropriately;

▌ they are empathic and sensitive to others' thoughts and feelings;

▌ they build alliances and connections in advance to support their case.

The essence of this characteristic is therefore the combination of two elements: planning in advance and sensitivity in action.

And finally, they have a deep concern for their impact. This means that they are constantly balancing two imperatives:

▌ taking actions that build the trust and respect of others; and

▌ worrying about, and being sensitive to, their impact and reputation.

The essence of this characteristic is a need to be respected and trusted rather than liked, combined with sensitivity to their reputation and impact.

Connected leaders know that only trust can give them the moral authority to lead at the 'real'.

THE LEADERSHIP TAKEAWAY

Here are the points from Chapter 5 that are pertinent to the way you think about leadership:

8. *Manage your trust account.*

Connected leaders know that they have a 'bank' of credibility with their stakeholders, a reserve of trust that can be drawn upon to get messages across or influence the way things are done. Their behaviour enables people to invest sufficient trust in them to allow them to lead the 'real' organization. Connected leaders do three things to manage their trust account actively:

- They become *trusted channels* by enabling the right information to flow to the right person. They are obsessive in leading this information flow.
- They exert *thoughtful influence* by ensuring that their actions are planned and take others' feelings and needs into action. They are obsessive in planning their interventions.
- They have a deep *concern for impact* by reflecting on how their actions will affect their trust account. They are obsessive about their reputation but are willing to take actions that may damage their popularity.

6

How to engage through meaning

Simon Fell has spent 29 years working in broadcasting, and what he doesn't know about the industry is not worth knowing. Simon is Controller of Emerging Technologies and Director of Technology for ITV's (Europe's largest commercial network) Consumer Division.

As a TV executive, he has had his fair share of glamour. He will recount the night he spent with Stanley Kubrick in his private recording studio. The film maker had, at the last minute, decided to hold up the US production of the *Full Metal Jacket* video as he disliked the sound quality. Because of his fear of flying, Kubrick was in the UK whilst production engineers were in the United States. Simon got a call from the United States, in the middle of the night, to go over to Kubrick's house and sort the sound out!

But glamour and the magic of television are not what attracted Simon to broadcasting; the magic of technology did. One of the most experienced engineers in the television industry, Simon has been immersed in digital television in the UK since before the start. He helped establish digital terrestrial and digital satellite television (he is member of the Digital Television Council, chairman of the Digital Television UK High Definition Forum and fellow of the Royal Television Society). In a world where, as he says, 'every viewer wants to pause everything', being able to capitalize on emerging and fast-changing technologies is critical to a network's survival. That Simon is recognized as having helped ITV to remain resilient to context change is to his credit. It is the way he has done it, however, that matters to aspiring connected leaders.

The questions this chapter will answer

▌ Why is meaning critical to performance?

▌ How do connected leaders co-create meaning?

WHY IS MEANING CRITICAL TO PERFORMANCE?

Simon's formal position requires him to be connected. To be successful, he needs the whole of ITV to embrace his ideas. Creating a new content distribution platform, for example, requires the input of production staff (mobile content cannot look like TV content). It requires engaging channel controllers (to be apprised of their plans). He requires financial backing and speed of execution. Yet Simon has no positional power over large parts of his stakeholder group (he does not control production, channel controllers or finance).

Meaning speeds up the execution

Crucially, he also knows that influencing the 'formal' structure to deliver takes more time than engaging the discretionary effort of the individuals residing within the 'real' organization. He also knows that, to rely on the 'formal' organization, you have to be able to codify and define any accountability you require of others for the accomplishment of a goal. The problem is, in Simon's world, you have no idea what you are going to require from others. All you know is that you want engaged employees who are going to work across the boundaries of the organization in order to respond to demanding customers' emerging needs.

His solution to engaging the parts his positional power cannot reach is to create a sense of shared meaning. Not only is meaning at the root of customers' motivational needs (as described in Chapter 1), but its co-creation is the only way fully to engage 'real' human performance in a sustainable way. Co-creating meaning ensures that a connected leader has an impact that will make people feel valued and involved. Meaning ensures that relationships have utility and reciprocity. Co-creating meaning with staff therefore enables leaders to achieve two things.

▌ First, it ensures the engagement of employees who, like customers, require the co-creation of meaning to engage with a community. To speed up a 'formal' organization operating in the warp-speed world of technology, media and telecommunications, Simon uses meaning to pit 'formal' incentives against 'real' obligations.

▌ Second, by co-creating meaning with employees, leaders ensure that 'formal' and 'real' objectives become aligned. Leaders are genuinely building the community on a solid internal basis rather than forcing employees to co-create with customers as a side issue necessary for the selling of goods and services. Co-creation of meaning becomes what we do around here.

Simon's vision

Simon is not what you might call an early adopter per se. He is not the kind to get the newest technology for its own sake. He is better described as a translator. Where early adopters see new technologies, Simon sees new possibilities. When he spotted that mobile technology was changing and that network operators were loosening their ties on what their users could have access to, the first thing Simon thought was: 'How can we play?' He knew that ITV could connect with its viewers in different ways. He could see that the technology would further the viewers' experience of programmes (and the advertising revenues). Many shows already relied on people calling in to vote for their favourite star or to answer questions on a quiz show. But Simon knew that, as mobile had revolutionized the way humans communicated, so it could revolutionize the way they thought about broadcasting.

His team was ready for the challenge. Together, they would bring new content, new revenue, new experiences and new capabilities to the market and ITV. Their vision was ambitious. Little did they know that, less than nine months after embarking on their journey with only the seed of an idea, Charles Allen, ITV's chief executive, would announce to a group of City analysts that Simon's new technological advances had become key drivers of ITV's future. Having insights is always satisfying but creating the future has to be the ultimate reward. That people want to engage in something bigger than them is something that we established in Chapter 1. But whilst plans and visions have made it as tools of business, meaning has still to reach the 'formal' dictionary. So how do you define meaning in a world of plans and visions?

Meaning versus plan and vision

Simon knows that technology is always put at either extreme of the vision/plan continuum. When early adopters or professionals think about technology, they are able to envision the future. They are quick to paint pictures that describe a world so removed from our everyday lives that it always sounds like a dream. On the other hand, bringing the dream to reality requires diligent work through a project plan. It is the clash of the culture of hype of technology salespeople and the culture of craft of the super-geeks that makes life difficult for most business people.

But neither the far-sightedness of a vision nor the short-term focus of a plan can do much to create sufficient meaning for the release of discretionary effort. Neither do much to help Simon engage the discretionary effort of his stakeholders. What he has learnt to do is to plug into their dreams rather than sell his.

When he meets viewers or potential users as well as colleagues whom he needs on board, Simon does not evangelize or share his vision. Nor does he just offer plans to the finance executives who will fund his ventures. Rather, he tries to move to a middle point where he makes technology accessible to their concerns. To the internal news team, for example, Simon did not pitch a 24/7 mobile news feed (that would be something only technology insomniacs would benefit from) nor did he try to give them a detailed project plan to bring news on mobile phones. What he did was simply to explain how his team's technology could contribute to the timely and accessible dispatch of news to a localized audience.

Think about it. Who cares about technology? Some news people do. But some news people are not enough to Simon. He wants all news people to care because he needs all news people to ask for the technology. So what is it that all news people care about? Answer: the dispatch of news in a timely and localized fashion. That's what they are passionate about.

Positioning system technology on mobile phones can ensure that only the news for the area you are in comes to your phone. OK, so maybe Simon is a clever spin doctor. Maybe he has the gift of the technology salesperson. Actually, yes, he is an expert spin doctor and, yes, he could sell anything to anyone and that is exactly what connected leaders are like. But they do so with integrity and honesty. Simon will not sell anything or spin a lie. He will always find the hook in something that is more concrete than a vision yet not as reductive as a plan. What matters to him is not the presentation of his problem (ie 'How do I get you to buy my technology?') but rather his audience's ability to contribute to the creation of a meaning relevant to them.

Individual versus organizational needs

Just as visions and plans operate on a continuum, so do individual and organizational needs. Whilst these can be aligned, they are often distinct. Creating meaning for an individual requires the leader to be able to bring together fully the individual and organizational agenda. How will fulfilling the organizational need help individuals fulfil their own inspirations? How will individuals pursuing their dreams help the organization achieve its goals? Answers to these questions have generally been provided in the form of economic incentives. In the case of individuals, the organization is prepared to give you money to explore your dreams (provided you do that off the job). In the case of individuals, I will help you provided you do not impact my life unnecessarily. In the people economy where the human 'being' rather than 'doing' or 'wanting' operates, this is no longer sustainable. Meaning cannot be replaced by a contract. Let's leave Simon for a moment – we'll come back to him later – and let me bring in James.

James works for a global utility company and is a specialist in site decommissioning. When a nuclear power plant closes, it can take up to 15 years for it to be safely decommissioned. The challenge for a plant leader on a decommissioning site is how to release the discretionary effort of people who are ultimately doing themselves out of a job. What James found on his arrival at a new site was that the previous management team's strategy had been less than transparent to the team. They set deadlines that were not met, with few or no consequences. They made promises that they did not keep. The result was complete mistrust in the leadership cadre and disengagement (not necessarily what one wants when handling a nuclear plant).

The reason I want to introduce James at this stage is because his story shows the difference between a connected leader working with meaning and dishonest spin doctoring or economic contracting. Like Simon with the news team, James decided that a vision was not the answer. Yet he could have easily proposed to be the safest and fastest decommissioning team or something to that effect – something that clearly he would have wanted. Nor did he give clarity through a plan ('We will have shut half the plant safely by such and such a date'). He could have done both and actually would have been successful in meeting his accountabilities because the only requirement placed on him by the organization was a safe and fast decommissioning completed by a certain date. But what James did was realize that individuals needed certainty rather than a plan or vision.

At the 'real' level, what was preoccupying the network was the search for certainty. 'Real' conversations revolved around that need. People worried not just about their jobs but about the impact the decommissioning would have on their community. To engage individuals in the organization's purpose, he had to give them certainty. From then on, no plan or vision could engage without fulfilling that need. James's solution was in fact really simple. He made sure that every proposed action would have to pass the clarity test: 'How is this removing uncertainty not just in the plant but in the community?' That was the meaning everyone would eventually get engaged around. It met both organizational and personal need. I have come to call what James did as using the meaning positioning system.

The meaning positioning system

Chapter 3 introduced the concept of leadership impact and in particular highlighted reciprocity as a key dimension. What Dave, Simon and James all show is that reciprocity requires clarity of meaning (ie 'What's the meaning of what we are trying to achieve to all of us?'). Clarity can be achieved through roles and rules but we know that, on their own, these would stop discretionary effort from being released, as the impact would be purely 'formal'. However, this positioning system is critical to the alignment of 'formal' and 'real' objectives. Right from the start of this book, I have mentioned the need for execution as well as agility if an organization wants to thrive. Formal accountabilities do matter. The organization does need focus. However, it is the balance between 'formal' accountabilities and 'real' reciprocity that matters. In James's case, working in the nuclear industry, there is a fine line between wanting your employees to shine (by working at the 'real') and letting them glow (because of a lack of accountabilities). Meaning provides the link between agility and execution.

What the connected leaders above do is engage their colleagues in dialogue to co-create meaning and a shared purpose that are unique to that organization (ie they take account of the requirement of the 'real'). In effect, they act like the satellite navigation system guiding individuals through the multiple individual and organizational layers of meaning along the organizational/personal (OP continuum) and plan/vision (PV continuum) axes. These axes are the longitude and latitude of an organization's meaning map.

The longitude and latitude of meaning

These two axes are dynamic. Organizations tend to gravitate along both continuums as markets and cultural concerns change – the organizational need tends to be overemphasized in downturns whilst visions are instruments usually deployed in times of growth. Both extremes, however, paralyse an organization. Each quadrant will bring with it its downfall.

Figure 6.1   The dimensions of meaning

Navigating towards the clarity point

To be effective in releasing discretionary effort to ensure healthy 'real' connections (ie connections that work to create communities of value to customers), leaders must navigate towards the clarity point of the meaning positioning system. The ultimate clarity point is found at the interception between the OP and PV continuums.

Figure 6.2   The meaning positioning system

The clarity point can move depending on the context the organization operates in. For example, personal needs might be put aside for the greater good of an organization under siege. Short-term organizational needs might be sacrificed to fulfil personal objectives for the retention of talent. But no one can constructively shift the clarity point without shifting the axis. In the first scenario, if people are prepared to let their needs go for the good of the organization, it requires agreement reached through dialogue. If the organization alone tries to move the clarity point towards the organizational need without discussing the impact on visions and plans, a vacuum will be created. Similarly, to embrace the visions and dreams of an individual will require a discussion around the implications for organizational outcomes. Dialogue becomes the key in shifting the axes (but more of that in Chapter 7).

Back to Simon, who as a connected leader needs to create a clarity point. Driving a corporate vision without taking individuals' personal needs into account would not have given traction to create the future. Focusing too much on helping others fulfil their needs with no regard for the organizational need would only have made Simon a good, but failing, networker. It is that relentless drive to find the clarity point that differentiates connected leaders from others. This they do by focusing on three sets of actions.

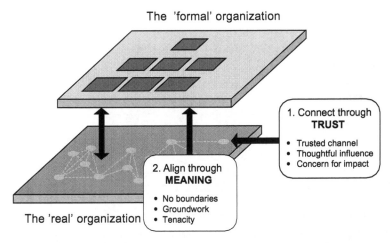

Figure 6.3   The leadership agenda, part 2

HOW DO CONNECTED LEADERS CO-CREATE MEANING?

To release discretionary effort in a way that achieves organizational objectives means driving towards the clarity point. To drive towards the clarity point means to be clear about what you mean! One thing that you will quickly notice when you speak to Simon is that passion pours out of him. He will speak for hours and show his excitement for things that could be. However, one of his crucible moments came in a discussion with Sir George Russell, who sits on the board of ITV. Having listened to one of Simon's displays of passion for an up-and-coming technology, Sir George took him aside and explained to him that he was talking a language no one else could understand. Sir

George didn't want him to translate his passion into other people's language (it might lose something in translation) but he needed him to build a shared language with others. Simon needed to let others in on the story. To facilitate the creation of meaning, Simon needed to do three things (see Figure 6.3):

▌ He needed to speak to everyone irrespective of function or level ('having no boundaries').

▌ He needed to do whatever it took to get others involved ('doing the groundwork').

▌ He needed to be patient and work diligently with others to write the story ('being tenacious').

Let me take each in turn.

HAVING NO BOUNDARIES

Boundaries define the 'formal'. Given the relentless pressure for personal delivery, to minimize external disruptions leaders have learnt to erect boundaries around their area of accountability. Yet boundaries, in so far as they cut across 'real' relationships, destroy the release of discretionary effort embedded in the organization and stand in the way of co-creation opportunities.

To call this characteristic 'no boundaries' is in fact a bit of a misnomer. Connected leaders do not ignore boundaries. They understand the need for 'formal' boundaries in enabling the focused delivery of objectives. They do not, however, view them as limits but rather as opportunities for relationships and dialogues. As the place where different agendas and needs collide, boundaries are the ideal places for the co-creation of meaning to happen. For connected leaders, boundaries indicate the points at which conversations need to be focused.

Creating meaning across boundaries

In both manner and speech, Simon is gentle. Yet to call him a diplomat would be doing him a disservice. Diplomacy implies too many compromises and often requires the type of sacrifices that delay time-critical projects.

When he and his team started to put together prototypes and drive forward their vision, they would step on a few toes. Others in ITV had been working on new technologies. The 'formal' agendas might have been different but the 'real' meaning was the same. Simon gathered a few teams together and opened his agenda to others. They could work together. Their priorities might be different (provide mobile technology for one show as opposed to create a corporate platform, for example) but the meaning and purpose (to bring TV outside the home) was the same.

Everywhere Simon spotted a 'competitive' initiative he saw an opportunity to 'cooperate'. He adopted a similar strategy to the open source movement, and others were invited to contribute. But as with the open source movement there are rules of conduct. Simon is clear: 'We do not work *for* you; we will work *with* you.' Making ownership joint ensured that outputs could not be retrofitted into the 'formal' structure.

Having no boundaries and the clarity positioning system

Despite a certain conservatism about personal impact (brought about by the careful management of their trust account), connected leaders are not smooth and mellow diplomats. Diplomats respect boundaries. They understand that their role is to influence carefully whilst staying within the laws and customs of the country they work in. Connected leaders on the other hand know that part of the reason they are so well connected is that they do not care about boundaries so much. You cannot establish 'real' connections in a 'formal' structure. 'This is my turf and that is yours' is a meaningless concept in the 'real' organization.

As we saw in Simon's story, whilst credibility matters to the building of trust, popularity is less important. Therefore connected leaders:

▌ take forceful action or use forceful language to assert their view;

▌ confront others openly if they feel standards are slipping;

▌ offer unsolicited feedback, advice and even criticism.

The essence of this characteristic rests in the sense of moral urgency that drives connected leaders to cross the implicit barriers people erect to make life run smoothly in the 'formal' organization (like territories, accountabilities, sensitivities and boundaries). Driving an organization towards the clarity point requires bringing diverging agendas together in a meaningful way.

Actions that undermine no boundaries

Connected leaders like Simon are brokers of clarity. They cut through the fog created by the multiple agendas present at the 'real' to help everyone co-create meaning and embrace a direction. For this reason, any reticence to engage would be counterproductive. Connected leaders cannot afford to be 'jobsworths', sticking to the rules at all costs, nor can they afford always to want to be liked.

However, this does not mean that connected leaders are cruel or aggressive. They do not fall for backbiting or disloyalty, persistently criticizing and undermining. They are not perceived as political animals (a common 'formal' occurrence) but rather as forceful contributors to the 'real' agenda. The difference between being perceived as an agent of the 'real' acting across 'formal' boundaries and a nuisance comes from connected leaders being sensitive to their environment. That sensitivity comes from the next characteristic: doing the groundwork.

DOING THE GROUNDWORK

Seeking the clarity point is all about getting stuck into 'real' conversations and doing the work necessary to get there. What differentiates connected leaders from others is that they do not need centre stage. In fact, they do not sit at the top of an organization dictating positions or ideas. They operate amongst the network and understand that their responsibility in the clarity positioning system is to ensure that the dialogues go smoothly. To do so, they act as facilitators of the process, undertaking glamorous and not-so-glamorous tasks.

Getting stuck in

The first time I met Simon was at a leadership retreat organized by ITV over two days. I had been talking to him and discussing leadership in the morning but it was only during lunch on the first day that I got to understand what Simon is really about.

The table at which he sat was particularly animated. Not only were people having fun, chatting and moving about but they were passing phones along the table, checking BlackBerries and generally oscillating between quiet awe and raucous laughter. Looking closer at the activity I realized that Simon was at the centre of it all. Not that everybody was looking at him – he wasn't the centre of attention per se. He was just orchestrating what was going on. He was in fact reprogramming every-one's phone to the ITV mobile pilot he and his team had launched.

The pilot was a kind of 'under the radar' project Simon's team thought they would try. They had organized content feeds and links. The portal they had created had everybody energized and excited. Simon, it turns out, had prepared for a product demo, yet no one felt they were taking part in a clever sales pitch. Simon was gently showing people how they could use this for their own benefit. He was noting down any actions they proposed or ideas they had. In other words, he had produced a prototype and was engaging in the co-creation of the product with the team around him. He was looking for the clarity point, letting the portal do the talking whilst he listened to their response. The key element in all this was that Simon had prepared. He wasn't standing in front of an audience with PowerPoint slides. He was the engineer reprogramming their phones.

Doing the groundwork and the clarity positioning system

It is worth making a distinction between what we commonly call net-working and connected leadership. Networking is primarily a 'formal' concern (designed to gain influence and build organizational awareness), whilst connected leadership is about working at the 'real' level to harness the flexibility of networks. Whilst being organized and systematic (ie doing the groundwork) does not necessarily distinguish the connected leader from less connected colleagues, it distinguishes the usefully con-nected leader from the idle networker.

Connected leaders are not afraid to roll their sleeves up and do both the preparation and the follow-up. They take care of some of the little things (which most leaders would describe as menial) that facilitate meetings and connections (eg reprogramming a phone or booking a room for a meeting). It is part of being credible. For connected leaders, their actions are about not just the connection itself, but what comes before and after. They recognize that you cannot navigate to the clarity point without being prepared to get inside the positioning system. To be effective, they need to be close to both the organizational and the individual need. In particular, connected leaders:

▌ are personally systematic, methodical and well organized;

▌ follow up on commitments and initiatives;

▌ get involved and do the little tasks that smooth things along.

The essence of this characteristic lies in the actions leaders take to support their need for connections. They ensure that interactions have the maximum benefit and go as smoothly as possible (in effect, connected leaders act as background facilitators). They understand that the process of bringing people together is a social process rather than a status-driven enterprise. They take pride in being thorough in their preparation and follow-up.

Actions that undermine doing the groundwork

Connected leaders are leaders. As such, they are not 'one of the team'. This is critical, as it would be wrong to assume that every relationship is one of friendship. As we have seen, the relationships are focused on credibility rather than popularity. However, doing the groundwork means that connected leaders do not fall for grandstanding, relying on other people to complete and finish tasks or ignoring the details.

The key to their credibility is that they do not break promises. They are organized, plan thoroughly and prepare their agenda. Doing the groundwork is what gives connected leaders the right to be tenacious.

BEING TENACIOUS

Imagine having to do the groundwork in a world as complex as the 'real' organization. Imagine being constantly pushed back as you cross boundaries. How soon do you give up? How much do you push? Connected leaders are resilient and patient to ensure they retain the capability to drive to the clarity point.

Push and pull

Simon has made his fair share of presentations to stakeholders. His laptop is loaded with presentations for audiences to listen to, whilst his bag is loaded with numerous gadgets (mobiles, iPods, etc) for them to play with. His laptop displays PowerPoint slides whilst he displays energy and infectious passion. Invariably he gets through the vision and the numbers without much noise from the audience. Technology is boring on paper, and hardened business leaders have had their fair share of pipe dreams with big numbers.

Simon knows that things take time to get done in organizations. But he also knows that, along the way, it's not just your organization you have to change but a few others too. When they started developing their new mobile service, Simon and the team were keen to get a technology partner they could work with. They tried to spec what they wanted with some of the major players in the business. They looked at the technologies available and how they could use them. They did due diligence work on a number of products and ideas. They could compromise on features. They could wait for development time. But they set themselves a rule: 'We will not compromise on our vision.' After each meeting and each review they would reconnect to their goal. As Simon says, 'We needed to keep meaning in our team and in ourselves to make sure we kept on going.'

They finally settled on a partner. It was neither the biggest nor the one with already established broadcasting technology. But it was the one that was the most open and exhibited the most latitude. They could have made the first step faster but that would not have guaranteed that they won the race.

Being tenacious and the clarity positioning system

Despite a reputation for being responsive and taking on board others' ideas, connected leaders stick with the task. Once a goal has been agreed, they pursue it to completion.

This does not, however, mean that connected leaders are narrow-minded. On the contrary, being tenacious necessitates flexibility. As Simon found out, connected leaders need to adopt different tactics as the situation requires. Sometimes, it means that they have to take the long view and pursue small steps in the right direction. You seldom see connected leaders sticking inflexibly to the same approach when it isn't working, but you do know that they will follow through. Connected leaders are therefore characterized by:

▌ tenacity – they keep coming back to the goal;

▌ flexibility in finding ways to achieve that goal;

▌ patience – being happy with incremental steps rather than potentially risky revolutions (which could damage their credibility).

In essence, this characteristic is the combination of the dogged pursuit of a goal with flexible tactics. Being single-minded will not give the ability to drive to the clarity point. Being tenacious will ensure that 'formal' and 'real' needs stay connected.

Actions that undermine being tenacious

Given the need for flexibility, there are a number of actions that will certainly undermine the effectiveness of connected leaders. If they fail to learn from experience or become overly reliant on edicts, they will narrow their options. Connected leaders also avoid shifting goals, single solutions, make-or-break gambles or big bangs. Whilst these may be appealing as simple strategies, they can only function in a 'formal' world where human beings are not free to deviate from established thinking patterns.

Because of their flexibility, connected leaders are not easily defeated, nor are they overhasty. It is critical for them to follow through rather than act as butterflies going from issue to issue.

What the connected leaders understand is that engaging the 'real' means creating a shared sense of clarity by finding shared meaning. To try to engage others by appealing only to individual needs and with no regard for 'formal' organizational objectives is a recipe for business failure. Once they have engaged the 'real' organization through meaning, they know that they need to make performance sustainable by linking 'real' desires to 'formal' objectives. This they do through dialogue. Paul, a director in a London stockbroking firm, will shed light on dialogue in Chapter 7.

THE 30-SECOND RECAP

To exploit fully the opportunities offered by the 'real' organization, connected leaders must facilitate the co-creation of meaning. The 'formal' organization has objectives and requirements. Its purpose is often expressed in visions (end states) and plans (road maps for actions). Individuals too have visions and plans. These are articulated in 'real' dialogues. Trying to align individuals to the 'formal' organization's vision will at best ensure that they put a minimal effort into the delivery of the plan, in so far as the economic incentive for doing so enables them to achieve their individual vision (remember Charlotte and her bedroom?). At worst, it will actively minimize discretionary effort as the meaning individuals seek cannot be accommodated.

To ensure that discretionary effort is released, connected leaders facilitate the co-creation of a shared meaning to give both the individual and the organization a sense of clarity. To do so, they rely on three characteristics.

First, they refuse to acknowledge the 'formal' boundaries as limits to dialogue. They:

▌ take forceful action or use forceful language to assert their view;

▌ confront others openly if they feel standards are slipping;

▌ offer unsolicited feedback, advice and even criticism.

The essence of this characteristic rests in the sense of moral urgency that drives connected leaders to cross the implicit barriers people erect to make life run smoothly in the 'formal'.

Second, they do the groundwork. In particular, connected leaders:

▌ are personally systematic, methodical and well organized;

▌ follow up on commitments and initiatives;

▌ get involved and do the little tasks that smooth things along.

The essence of this characteristic is in the action leaders take to support their talk of connections.

And finally, they are tenacious in their pursuit of the clarity point. Connected leaders are therefore characterized by:

▌ tenacity – they keep coming back to the goal;

▌ flexibility in finding ways to achieve that goal;

▌ patience – being happy with incremental steps rather than potentially risky revolutions (which could damage their credibility).

In essence, this characteristic is the combination of the dogged pursuit of a goal with flexible tactics.

Connected leaders understand that the alignment of the individual's vision and the organization's objective can come only from the co-creation of a shared meaning. To co-create meaning in the 'real' is the only way to ensure the organization remains agile in the delivery of its 'formal' objectives.

THE LEADERSHIP TAKEAWAY

Here are the points from Chapter 6 that are pertinent to the way you think about leadership:

9. *Switch on your clarity positioning system.*

Connected leaders understand that to engage individuals fully (ie release their discretionary effort) they need to operate in the 'real' organization. They know that their role is not to dictate a 'formal' agenda but rather to harness the 'real' organization's flexibility to deliver the 'formal' objectives. To do so, they need to create a clarity point at the junction between an individual's vision and plans and the organization's vision and plans. This clarity point can only be found through the co-creation of meaning. Connected leaders do three things to encourage the co-creation of the clarity point:

- They have no boundaries in the way they operate across the organization, recognizing only the opportunities for relationships. They are obsessive about navigating in the 'real'.
- They act as facilitators of clarity by doing the groundwork to ensure that everything is in place for relationships to flourish. They are obsessive about making things happen.
- They see setbacks only as opportunities for being tenacious. They do understand the need for long-term sustainable impact. They are obsessive about co-creating clarity.

7

How to sustain performance through dialogue

When Paul, a director in a stockbroking firm, called to ask me to facilitate one of his team meetings, I never thought that one day I would be writing about the experience. His request was not extraordinary. The meeting was the first of his new team. His firm had merged with another and, along with his original six direct reports, three new team members had joined. The objective of the meeting was 'to shape the newly formed function's strategy and formulate a plan'.

Prior to the meeting, I met individually with team members to go over their expectations. Not surprisingly, the new team members were anxious. They expected that they were about to be told what to do. The members of Paul's old team on the other hand were jubilant. 'We need to do what we did before. After all, we have taken over their firm, so we must have been doing something right', they told me.

There is nothing uncommon about what transpired during that meeting. You will have had similar experiences and frustrations during your meetings. It is what Paul did that makes the event worth retelling.

The questions this chapter will answer

▎ Why does real dialogue matter to performance?

▎ How do connected leaders sustain dialogue?

WHY DOES REAL DIALOGUE MATTER TO PERFORMANCE?

Meetings are all about dialogue. Or are they? Most forms of communication in organizations are designed to influence people towards a specific outcome. People may speak and may even be heard, but are they actually listened to? Paul's meeting typified the difference between influencing and dialogue. In the people economy, where trust is critical to the co-creation of meaning, the difference between influencing and dialogue is the difference between failure and success. Dialogue maintains warmth in a relationship. It also ensures that a relationship with a connected leader is low-maintenance. Above all, in terms of the levers of connected leadership (ie the things leaders do to release discretionary effort that will maintain the connections necessary to the creation of communities of value), dialogue helps them drive to the clarity point. Dialogue enables them to maintain the alignment of the 'real' connections to the 'formal' objectives.

Influencing is not about the co-creation of meaning; dialogue is. As Paul found out in a grey room on the third floor of a typical stockbrokers' office in the City of London on a sunny July day, dialogue is about real conversations, and these require leaders to act differently. Here is what happened.

Mapping conversations

As I arrived for the meeting, I could hear conversations coming from the coffee station outside the room. People were polite, talking about what they had done at the weekend and making 'small talk'. As they entered the meeting room however, the atmosphere changed.

I had agreed with Paul that he would open the meeting, introduce the agenda and hand over to me once he had explained my role. Whilst he was doing this, I prepared a conversation map. This is a simple tool I always use when working with groups. On a piece of paper, I draw the table and indicate the position of everyone in the room. When anyone speaks I trace a line going from that person to whomever the person is talking to. Often the lines end up going to more than one person. Sometimes, some people have no lines going out but a few lines coming in.

As is often the case, the meeting started with a lot of lines going from Paul to others. He was, after all, introducing the meeting. A few people made remarks about the agenda. The conversation was not so much flowing as going back and forth between Paul and a couple of his colleagues. Before we began to tackle the main part of the agenda, I summed up the expectations people had expressed and asked for input on the agenda. It was at that stage that my conversation map started to look strange.

Dialogues of the deaf

Everyone started to talk. New members expressed some of their concerns at not knowing the norms of the acquiring organization (eg 'How are things done around here?', 'How do we get input?'). Old members expressed concerns at the potential derailment that could result from the merger (eg 'We have done this well and we should continue along existing tracks'). The map was filling up with lines coming from all around the table, but the lines were all landing in the middle of the table. Just as the meeting would have done if it had carried on in this way, the lines were going nowhere.

In France there is a saying that describes what was happening at Paul's meeting. We call it *un dialogue de sourds* (dialogue of the deaf). Everybody speaks but no one listens.

Dialogues of the deaf frequently occur in organizations. Everybody around the table is trying to influence others towards a specific outcome. Therefore, when someone is talking, someone else concentrates on finding the next line of argument. No one builds on anyone else's points. The best you can hope is for your point to be hijacked to support someone else's point. Consequently, no point ever gets built on, reshaped or transformed into an ideal solution. Such discussions can never lead to the clarity point. What the French call a dialogue of the deaf, clinical psychologists call paranoia. Paranoid people look for every bit of information in everything they hear that they can twist to fit their view of reality and as a result are unable to confront any scenario outside that view – however real this might be. Paranoia is a 'formal' disease.

Paul himself went for the ultimate dialogue of the deaf (aided by a PowerPoint presentation). He asked initially for opinions and thoughts, but then brought out a deck of slides with his preconceived view about what should be done. How often do you ask for a brainstorm and get out the answer at the end using the magic words 'Interestingly, I did a bit of thinking beforehand and I think you covered all the points I have' – irrespective of what they said?

The inevitable outcome of influence

If we use the 'meaning positioning system' introduced in the previous chapter, Paul saw his role in the meeting as providing clarity through plans and visions rather than co-created meaning. For this reason, he had to act as an evangelist for his plan. Leaders (personalized leaders especially) tend to see themselves as evangelists. In their view, people need certainty and therefore corporate truth. Like any other religious truth, the corporate truth needs evangelists to spread the word enthusiastically and create converts. The truth does not change – it is convincing people of its appeal that creates value.

The only real improvement to this strategy since biblical times has been a tactical one. Leaders now have more technology to ensure that the word spreads. They can choose influencers and target viral campaigns that make the truth travel at high speed. Such tactical improvements might make the truth more palatable or might even blind people to the availability of any other truths, but they do not in themselves make the necessary leap to capture emotional engagement. Evangelists do not need dialogue; they need only authoritatively expressed convictions. Paul needed, he thought, to influence decisions rather than to impact meaning. The consequences of evangelism can be adherence to a faith. However, in a world that requires full engagement on the part of employees so that they freely create the connections necessary to the creation of communities of value to self-actualizing individuals, it will fail to deliver discretionary effort targeted at the delivery of a common objective.

Storytellers and evangelists

Contrast the role of evangelists to what Gary did when he talked about his father rescuing a customer, Dave when he talked about his childhood in Liverpool, or Simon when he talks about technology helping the delivery of a better experience and you begin to see a different dynamic – that of storytelling.

Connected leaders use their influence differently. They create stories that make people want to belong, not just images that might help them obey. They build real conversations – ones that allow people to speak and be heard. The religious analogy is useful here, as there cannot be two versions of the truth; either the sacred text is the word of God, or it isn't. Whilst this may be so, religious followers the world over, just like human beings in the people economy, are engaged in conversations to find meaning: they co-create not the basic tenets of the faith but the way that they, as individuals, can live within them (they look for the clarity point, explained in Chapter 6, at the intersection of the religious precepts and their individual ability to live by them). Followers connect at the 'real' through the co-creation of clarity to ensure they meet the 'formal' objectives of their faith.

The key to engaging with stakeholders, gaining their trust and co-creating meaning is to create insights. The leader's plot line might still carry the day but such dialogue ensures richer characters. In the people economy, evangelists are no longer enough. Self-actualizing individuals no longer require just a set of beliefs. They also need sources of ideas to enable the co-creation of meaning. Co-creation of meaning can only happen at the 'real' level (ie through relationships). Stories are the language of relationships and therefore the language of the 'real'. Dialogues are power plays that underpin stories. But power in this context means something different from the failed influencing that was happening in Paul's meeting.

Dialogue as power play

In Paul's meeting, power was personalized. It was about one individual having power over another. Paul derived his power from his hierarchical position. His original direct reports derived theirs from their long-term association with Paul. The latter is the least mature form of power, best demonstrated by the school playground saying, 'My daddy is bigger than yours.'

The type of power used in a dialogue or real conversation is different. It is assertive and interdependent. Each party to the dialogue can agree or disagree, but both aim to impact and influence the other for a common growth goal rather than an exercise in personal aggrandizement. The purpose of the dialogue is to make each other stronger, in contrast to conventional influencing where one party conforms to the wishes of the other. The former is done through the act of co-creation (the building and shaping of ideas). The aim of a real dialogue is to arrive at a shared understanding rather than an agreed way forward. At the core of any dialogue therefore lie a number of dynamics for which there is no single linear causal relationship between outcome and related dialogue.

What happens when power changes

To shift from evangelizing to storytelling is fundamentally to change the nature of power. In storytelling mode, the leader relies on others' input. The story is created by the interaction. The role of storyteller shifts from the leader to the follower as the act of co-creation evolves. Power is shared.

As Paul's meeting progressed, it was clear that power was changing hands but it was not changing in nature. The new members were becoming more aggressive in their input (personalized power has a tendency to beget personalized power). They were making strong points about the strengths that they brought to the new merged firm. They forcefully argued that, whilst their firm might have been taken over, their function was the stronger of the two in the marketplace.

For the meeting to move forward and achieve Paul's desired emotional engagement, power no longer needed to shift around the room. Instead, it needed to change in nature. I asked Paul to tell us the story of the takeover. I told him that I wasn't interested in the economic rationale behind the move but rather in the story behind the headlines. What were leaders thinking when they made the first move? What were their fears? What were their expectations and desires for the deal? As he talked, Paul's identity shifted from that of the positional leader to that of the executive facing tough decisions. The dynamic started to change.

It would be easy to ignore the unease in the room and say that everything went smoothly thereafter but it didn't. For a while it was strange. Some participants even looked embarrassed at hearing about the doubts and dreams of executives higher up the corporate echelon as they embarked on the deal. But this natural apprehension at the discovery of humanity in the midst of the corporate beast quickly evaporated. The new members spoke about their apprehensions in the early stages of the deal. They outlined how they were getting ready to leave. A few jokes were made about what each team thought the other one was like, and suddenly a shared identity started to emerge through the dialogue, enabled by the story of the takeover.

Dialogue and people economy performance

Clearly, a stockbroking firm in the City of London is hardly a place for 'soft' approaches or 'fluffy' experiments. The story enabled Paul to move around Chapter 4's leadership matrix from personalized to connected leader via authentic leadership. When Paul told the story, he precipitated an act of co-creation that led to engagement.

We all view the world through a set of filters (the models we have in our minds). Every problem or opportunity is tainted by these filters. Our education shapes our views and the higher we climb the corporate ladder the more our views are reinforced and become entrenched. This is not surprising, given the CEO disease (ie honest feedback becomes harder to come by the more senior we get). Asking Paul to explain his story was therefore not a 'soft' experiment; it was simply a way of engineering a power shift by altering others' mental models (it enabled participants to understand the emotional assumptions and drivers behind decisions). The roles that people had given each other (and accepted) were dictated by the 'formal' organization. The meeting was shaped around new and old members, direct reports and director, winners and losers in the takeover. The source of power was positional and its outcome 'formal'. As the meeting was 'formal', the outcome was always going to be adversarial. 'Formal' dynamics are adversarial by nature, as they are defined by boundaries. In that context, there was no way Paul would ever achieve his stated objective. He could not execute his plan and ask for discretionary effort to be targeted at the creation of connections. The only way to gain that engagement was to move away from a 'dialogue of the deaf' to a real conversation.

Connected leaders make that shift and create real conversations in order to sustain performance. They do so by using three key characteristics. It is these that I want to introduce.

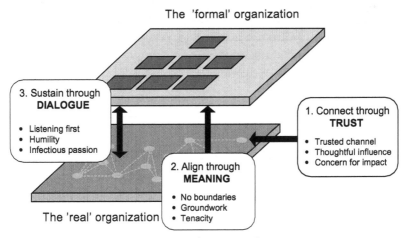

Figure 7.1   A complete picture of the leadership agenda

HOW DO CONNECTED LEADERS SUSTAIN DIALOGUE?

Real conversations that drive people to the clarity point require two parties to engage in dialogue. The role of the leader is to have an impact that ensures others take part in the creation of connections to facilitate the building of communities of value. It is often assumed that actions are required in order for an outcome to happen. For example, in the case of dialogue, leaders think that, by asking questions or soliciting input, conversations will be generated.

This is not entirely true. In practice, actions alone do not generate outcomes, but interactions do (ie the leader's intent is of little value unless aligned with the follower's perception). To create interactions, in a strange way, the first step is not to speak but to listen.

LISTENING FIRST

I highlighted the action Paul took by talking about the takeover story as being the turnaround point from a 'dialogue of the deaf' to a real conversation. However, the very fact that I had to ask Paul to change tack highlights his failure to listen. Whilst he was busy shaping his influencing strategy he could not hear the destructive interventions made by others around the table. He could not engage them in a conversation. In effect, he was not spotting the lines landing in the middle of the table. The only reason I was able to ask him to change his approach was that I had been acting as his ears. I deserve no special credit for this. I was not involved in the dialogue. I was an observer. It is that capacity to be involved in the content of the conversation yet detached enough to observe its process that sets connected leaders apart.

Deafening silence

When asked how he approached conversations, one of the connected leaders I talked to said 'By treating them as deafening silences.' What he meant was that conversations happen on two levels: 'what is being said' and 'why it is being said'. It is the latter that matters to the co-creation of meaning, yet it is the part that is never spoken (ie the deafening silence). It is that part of the conversation that a leader can only spot by listening for the silence that punctuates the conversation. Most people would do well to ask themselves 'For whose benefit am I going to say what I am about to say?' but, for connected leaders, finding the answer to that question is critical. Are people making an intervention for the purpose of self-aggrandizement? Are they making the intervention to make others feel weak? Are they talking to fill in the void they are afraid others may fill with their ideas? Understanding the unspoken intent of others is key to building a real conversation.

Listening first and real conversations

But connected leaders do not ask for feedback. There is a vital difference between listening first and seeking feedback. Asking for feedback means that you already know what you want and are willing to accept deviations and tweaks. Listening first means wanting other people to help build the ideas in the first place – a precondition to finding the clarity point. Connected leaders often approach an issue without a predetermined position, asking questions and gathering data. This does not mean that they do not have a view, but they understand that, given the power of multiple mental models, their own view can be only of limited value.

They are valued by their colleagues because they are receptive but also because they can be vehicles for their ideas – more effective carriers and persuaders, perhaps, than the individuals themselves. Observing connected leaders in dialogue means seeing:

▊ fewer preconceived strategies, developed without others' input, than with other leaders;

▊ a willingness to adopt and champion other people's ideas;

▊ a reputation as approachable and for opening doors for people.

The essence of the listening-first characteristic is about genuinely seeking, championing and using other people's ideas and input.

Actions that undermine listening first

It is in this context that true conversations develop. Connected leaders shy away from grand designs. By working with others, they avoid making decisions in isolation. Whilst they use others' ideas, they always give credit to the originator of the idea. This ensures that their trust accounts remain intact.

Connected leaders never refuse to listen or adapt. They have only minimal attachment to their own ideas in so far as they will never fall for staged consultations and leading or rhetorical questions. They know full well that this kind of manoeuvring seldom leads to real engagement. Listening first, however, presupposes that you believe others have something of value to say. Building resilience to context change through dialogue therefore requires an ability to show enough humility for others to feel they can engage in the conversation.

HUMILITY

Lack of humility is easily explained yet increasingly hard to justify. The brain weighs about 1.5 kilos. It comprises millions of neurons. Each neuron can make numerous connections and pathways to other neurons. Pyotr Anokhin, a student of Ivan Pavlov (of salivating dogs fame), published a research paper in 1968 comparing the human brain to 'a keyboard on which hundreds of millions of different melodies – acts of behaviour or intelligence – can be played at once'.[1] He established that the total number of potential neural connections is equal to 1 followed by 10.5 million kilometres of standard typewritten zeros.[2] It's hard to show humility when you possess such a powerful instrument designed to give you an edge over others.

The person you report to is 72.8 per cent water

I am not a biologist and I don't know the person to whom you report. So I will leave it up to you to research what the other 27.2 per cent is. But whilst the brain is indeed capable of marvellous things, not one person, however good a leader he or she is, will have the answers to all the problems an organization is likely to encounter. Even if the search for intelligence is real (in the United States alone, in one year in the 1980s, over 500 million standardized IQ tests were administered to children and adults[3]), irrespective of how intelligent he or she is, one person cannot handle the ever-increasing sum of human knowledge. Our collective intelligence has created a world that is simply too complex for our individual intellectual capabilities to make full sense of.

Add the fact that our brains have seemingly unlimited potential to a constantly increasing knowledge base combined with technical specialization, and a major leadership challenge emerges. The more we know, the more competitors invent, and the less we comprehend. The US Patent Office opened for business in 1790 with three patents on its books. By 1900 it had assigned 700,000 and by 2000 around 10 million.[4] Despite the commissioner's famous prediction in 1899 that 'everything that can be invented has been invented', human ingenuity does not cease to push back the boundaries of knowledge. In this context, to feel that one has the answer to all the problems an organization is likely to face can only lead to disaster.

Humility and real conversations

Our customers are smart. Our employees are smart. Our competitors are smart. The days of trying to find a leader to outsmart all of them are over. Success now depends on the leader's ability to capture the entire wealth of knowledge and imagination the organization has to offer. As we have seen, only a focus on the 'real' can release this wealth. Therefore, dialogue (the language of the 'real') offers the ability to engage the full ingenuity (intelligence and imagination) of people. So, how does humility create the emotional connections necessary for dialogue to happen?

It drives connected leaders to rely on others, creating relationships and bonds. It enhances the approachability and receptiveness that their colleagues value so highly and gives them the right to participate in the 'real'. It sets an example for others and generates two-way connections. Connected leaders most certainly don't know it all, but they know someone who does. They:

- are honest with themselves and others about limits to their expertise and knowledge (they know when to ask for help);

- admit where necessary to mistakes and error;

- seek support, rope in colleagues to help and look for experts to advise them.

The essence of humility lies in the genuine reciprocity it generates. Connected leaders both seek and offer assistance. As a result, they create enduring connections that prove useful as the context changes.

Actions that undermine humility

If humility brings about a shift in dynamics, the characteristics displayed by many leaders today stop that shift. In fact, as in Paul's meeting, the very nature of today's organizational conversations creates a humility-destroying vicious cycle. These pseudo-conversations generate in most leaders a feeling of helplessness, which they try to remedy through greater personal involvement, influence and achievement. In effect, the more the dialogue fails, the more they display power to influence and the more the dialogue will fail.

As a result of this cycle, many leaders go it alone. They reject support, papering over the cracks (seeing a need for support as a failure to influence). Mistakes are hidden and knowledge and contributions overplayed. It is this overconfidence and need to play the part of a guru that ensure the disempowerment of those around them. Connected leaders balance their needs and do not overcompensate. They do not, for example, seek help unnecessarily nor do they accept indecision, as this would lead to dishonesty and therefore damage trust. What sustains them in the balancing act between humility and action is their refusal of pessimism. In that way, connected leaders need the third characteristic of dialogue. They need passion that is infectious.

INFECTIOUS PASSION

Like humility, infectious passion is an attractor of people and a creator of connections. Whilst the idea that optimism influences our desire to engage in dialogue is reinforced by developments in psychology and neuroscience, you do not require a degree to understand it. Ask yourself the question 'Who do I turn to most often?' The answer in some way, shape or form is likely to involve passion. Passion is a highly contagious infection. It is not necessary for leaders to take any action to create an infection; they only need to display authoritative passion.

Passion + authority = infection

If passion provides the thrust to the infection, authority is the vector that ensures it spreads. Authority means that the passion is well founded and articulated. Connected leaders are not bubbly, gregarious cheerleaders;

they have a focused, calm passion. Going back to Gary, Dave and Simon it is clear that their passion informs their actions. What makes them authoritative is their deep knowledge of their business and an ability to articulate that knowledge.

Synchronizing thoughts, words and deeds sustains an authoritative approach. In that way the passion displayed by connected leaders is more mature than a mindless enthusiasm or hobby. Projecting that passion authoritatively encourages others to believe in the possible. Passion creates a 'reality-altering field' around the leader. People who experience the passion of connected leaders are not taken in by lies or dreams; they trust the leader's passion and become infected because they know that the articulation of it makes sense. It may not yet be reality but the synchronicity provides them with the reassurance that the leader is prepared, in Chuck Jones's words, to 'choose the hill and die on it'. The creation of a mindset of possibilities (or at least the removal of cognitive obstacles to new approaches) makes dialogue possible. As the passion is articulated it can be built on.

Passion is not cheerfulness. Cheerfulness is a state of mind that cannot by itself create dialogue. It is not something others can build on. It may make them cheerful but it does not provide them with the opportunity to explore a common meaning. Being passionate on the other hand presupposes a depth that can be explained, challenged, supported and explored, providing the foundations for co-creation. It is humility that keeps infectious passion in check, stopping it from becoming mindless bullying.

Infectious passion and real conversations

This ability to infect others with the thought that something can be done raises others' enthusiasm and commitment to remain within the conversation. To make dialogue possible, connected leaders express their appreciation of others and put forward their passion authoritatively. In practice, observing connected leaders is seeing them:

▊ believing fervently in the power of the organization and acting on this belief;

▊ being generous with their time and in their opinion of others.

The essence of this characteristic lies in the warmth and humanity that connected leaders put into their working relationships.

Actions that undermine infectious passion

Infectious passion is easily contrasted with bitterness, suspicion and defeatism, which have become all-too-common characteristics of 'formal', 'Dilbert' dialogues and approaches. It does not however mean unfounded optimism. Connected leaders do not ignore obvious flaws and difficulties. They will not gloss over others' concerns. Flaws and difficulties as well as concerns are all exposed and addressed. It would be wrong to equate connected leaders with leaders who ignore reality or hard facts.

What connected leaders understand is that, for the flaws, concerns and hard facts to surface, the environment must be such that the conversation is allowed to flow. This requires the ability to engage at a human level, which is what the infectious passion provides.

What the dialogue characteristics demonstrate, even more than any of the other connected leader characteristics, is the need to have a multidimensional approach to our development as leaders. It is not enough to develop a set of tactics and actions. As we have seen, impact and power shifts require a change in our understanding of what leadership is and our mindset about what makes this effective. Development goals are required at a number of levels. How you think is important and what you do matters, yet a more fundamental shift needs to occur. As we saw in Chapter 4, connected leadership can only be developed through a radical rethink of who we are as leaders and what drives us. This requires us to undertake the hard task of recognizing the models that shape who we are as leaders. This is where Part 4 takes us and where the BaMbuti tribe of the Ituri forest can help.

THE 30-SECOND RECAP

Connected leaders rely on dialogue to sustain the performance gained by operating at the 'real'. Dialogue ensures the co-creation of meaning and reinforces trust. Yet, whilst many conversations happen in organizations, most can be described as 'dialogues of the deaf' – many people speak but no one listens. Organizational conversations are more akin to influencing exchanges than to true dialogues. People try to convince each other by appealing to a number of rational arguments that satisfy their mental models.

Leaders have become evangelists of their own truth but do not understand why people are not converting to their view. The boundaries of the 'formal' organization necessary to the evangelist are the very boundaries that limit the effectiveness of evangelism as a source of emotional engagement. Connected leaders are storytellers not evangelists. They create narratives that enable others to reconnect with their humanity and invite them to invest emotionally in the search for shared meaning, thereby ensuring their complete performance. To do so, connected leaders adopt three key characteristics.

They listen first. This means that they have:

▍ fewer preconceived strategies, developed without others' input, than other leaders;

▍ a willingness to adopt and champion other people's ideas;

▍ a reputation as approachable and for opening doors for people.

The essence of the listening-first characteristic is about genuinely seeking, championing and using other people's ideas and input.

They display humility. This means that they:

▍ admit to themselves and others to limits in their expertise and knowledge (they know when to ask for help);

▍ admit where necessary to mistakes and errors;

▍ seek support, rope in colleagues to help and look for experts to advise them.

The essence of this characteristic lies in the genuine reciprocity it generates. Connected leaders both seek and offer assistance. As a result, they create enduring connections that will prove useful as the context changes.

And finally, they possess an infectious passion, which means that they:

▍ believe fervently in the power of the organization and act on this belief;

▍ are generous with their time and in their opinion of others.

The essence of this characteristic lies in the warmth and humanity that connected leaders put into their working relationships.

Connected leaders know that dialogue is the only 'real' instrument able to sustain the co-creation of meaning enabled by trust that will ensure performance and resilience to context change.

THE LEADERSHIP TAKEAWAY

Here are the points from Chapter 7 that are pertinent to the way you think about leadership:

10. *Create dialogues.*

Connected leaders know that dialogue is necessary to sustain the performance-enhancing relationships that the 'real' organization offers. They understand that stories are the language of relationships. Their behaviour is directed at creating the conditions necessary for others to engage in dialogues that co-create meaning. Connected leaders do three things actively to create dialogue opportunities:

- They listen first by ensuring that they are receptive to the process as well as the content of the conversation. They are obsessive in trying to understand why people say what they say.
- They display humility by being receptive to others' input as they understand their own limits. They are obsessive about generating genuine reciprocity.
- They have an infectious passion that draws others in by authoritatively expressing boundless belief in the potential of the 'real' organization. They are obsessive about the potential value afforded by the humanity that resides inside the organization.

Diagnostic tools 3:

How connected are you?

HOW CONNECTED ARE YOU?

If impact is the output of leadership and beliefs are the inputs, then trust, meaning and dialogue turn input into output. Rating yourself against these three dimensions (ie trust, dialogue and meaning) will give you insights on how your leadership actions help or hinder you in your pursuit of leadership impact.

The following exercise has been designed to measure how often you display each of the characteristics. First, complete the exercise yourself. This will measure your intent. Of course, as I have noted throughout this book, what really matters to a leader's effectiveness is not so much the leader's intent as the leader's impact (ie as rated by others' perception). I would therefore encourage you to get others to complete the questionnaire, reflecting on what they see you do. Having both pictures will enable you to raise your level of self-awareness and target any development activity appropriately.

To complete this exercise, consider each statement, given the proposition 'The person I am thinking of' (either yourself or the person who has asked you to complete the questionnaire) followed by the relevant statement. Place a mark in the box on the frequency scale that best represents your experience.

	never		rarely		often		always
1. is in the middle of the organization s information flow.							
2. is sensitive to ensure his/her reputation.							
3. is careful in planning his/her contribution.							
4. is not afraid to get stuck in doing small tasks that help.							
5. involves others in the development of strategies.							
6. takes forceful actions to assert his/her view.							
7. knows what I need to know and what I don t.							
8. admits his/her mistakes.							
9. is focused on the goal.							
10. is generous with his/her opinions of others.							
11. confronts others openly if standards are slipping.							
12. is flexible enough to change tactics to achieve the goal.							
13. is always pointing out new ways for me to grow.							
14. does not aim for potentially damaging revolutions.							
15. offers unsolicited advice, feedback or criticisms.							
16. is systematic and methodical.							
17. takes actions to build trust and respect.							
18. seeks support and help from others who know more.							
19. champions other people s ideas.							
20. is sensitive to the way he/she is perceived.							
21. follows up on commitments and initiatives.							
22. thinks about the impact he/she will have on others.							
23. builds alliances to support his/her case.							
24. speaks well of the organization.							
25. is approachable and opens doors for others.							
26. makes time to support others.							
27. is open about the limits of his/her abilities.							

Having completed the questionnaire, add up each of your results in the scoring template below. Any answer in the never box scores zero. Moving in incremental steps of 1, give yourself a top score of 6 for any score in the always box.

26. makes time to support others.

| 0 | 1 | 2 | 3 | 4 | 5 | 6 |

TRUST LEVER

statement 1		statement 7		statement 13		Total score	
	+		+		=		Trusted channel

statement 3		statement 22		statement 23		Total score	
	+		+		=		Thoughtful influence

statement 17		statement 20		statement 2		Total score	
	+		+		=		Concern for impact

MEANING LEVER

statement 6		statement 11		statement 15		Total score	
	+		+		=		No boundaries

statement 16		statement 21		statement 4		Total score	
	+		+		=		Doing the groundwork

statement 9		statement 12		statement 14		Total score	
	+		+		=		Tenacious

DIALOGUE LEVER

statement 5		statement 19		statement 25		Total score	
	+		+		=		Listening first

statement 27		statement 8		statement 18		Total score	
	+		+		=		Humility

statement 24		statement 10		statement 26		Total score	
	+		+		=		Infectious passion

Having added up your scores, you can shade the boxes below to get a graphical representation of your scores.

TRUST	0	5	9	13	18
Trusted channel					
Thoughtful influence					
Concern for impact					

MEANING	0	5	9	13	18
No boundaries					
Doing the groundwork					
Tenacious					

DIALOGUE	0	5	9	13	18
Listening first					
Humility					
Infectious passion					

Interpreting your results

The characteristics described under each connected leadership lever enable you to develop a connected impact. Any characteristic you have that scores less than 9 represents an area of concern. Either people do not see you take the actions necessary to establish that characteristic often enough or you are still at a stage where you exhibit only part of the characteristic.

It is important to compare the profile you have completed with the profile others have completed on your behalf. For any characteristic where you score more than 9 and others have scored you less than 9, your intent does not translate into impact. You want to give examples of when you feel you displayed the behaviour to others and seek feedback from them. Conversely, if they have scored you higher than you have, you will need to gather examples from them to understand where the difference between your and their view came from.

You should also see a correlation between the characteristics above and the five areas of impact introduced in Chapter 3 although, as we will discover in Part 4, the correlation is not as strong as could be imagined, as I have simplified the relationship between impact and characteristics for the purpose of clarity in Part 3. However, fear not, I shall reintroduce the complexity in Part 4 (but complexity does not have to be complicated)!

Next steps

When trying to develop behavioural characteristics, it is important to understand at what level of the iceberg model (introduced in Chapter 4) the development needs to happen. We fail to demonstrate certain characteristics for a number of reasons. Maybe it is something we do not know how to do (a skills issue) or maybe it is not something we recognize as important to our role (a role perception issue) or maybe we simply do not feel energized by it (a motivation issue). Each of these will require a different development or coping strategy.

Part 4 of the book, the final part, will walk you through the process of building a targeted and focused connected leadership development plan.

Part Four

Developing connected leadership

Famed anthropologist Colin Turnbull tells the following story of Kenge, a 22-year-old Pygmy from the BaMbuti tribe on his first venture outside his native Ituri forest:

> Kenge looked over the plains and down to where a herd of about a hundred buffalo were grazing some miles away. He asked me what kind of insects they were, and I told him they were buffalo, twice as big as the forest buffalo known to him. He laughed loudly and told me not to tell such stupid stories... he then tried to liken the buffalo to the various beetles and ants with which he was familiar. He was still doing this when we got into the car and drove down to where the animals were grazing. He watched them getting larger and larger, and though he was as courageous as any Pygmy, he moved over and sat close to me and muttered that it was witchcraft.[1]

Brought up in the dense forest, Kenge lived in a close-up, vertical world. Having never seen the horizon, he did not have a concept of perspective. We are all Kenges. We have all grown up in the dense, close-up, vertical world of the 'formal' organization. Employees talk about career ladders, whilst customers want to escalate complaints. The language of business is the language of heights. To develop connections, we need impact. To have impact, we need to change our beliefs through actions. But how do we start? How do we develop a new perspective? Part 4 offers the five development stages necessary to leaders wanting the road map to climb down the 'formal' heights and see what is happening in the 'real' plains.

There are five steps to the development of connected leadership. Of course, the diagnostic tools throughout this book should have given you a pretty good understanding of your current situation. Part 4 is designed to help you map out a development strategy. The five steps described here are as shown below.

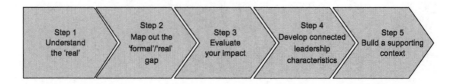

Together, these five steps ensure that your efforts are targeted at the different levels of effectiveness. Following them will enable you to travel through the iceberg model introduced in Chapter 4. They will also ensure that you not only develop your capability but also address the organizational issues that need to be aligned to your customer leadership strategy.

Step 1:

Understand the 'real'

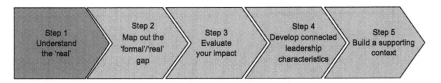

Figure 8.1 Connected leadership development, step 1

An agile organization is one where the informal connections and interactions (the 'real' instruments) support the realization of your 'formal' efforts.

Throughout this book, the underpinning assumption has been that connections are a good thing in general and that, in the people economy, the more connections the better. In Chapters 1 and 2 I introduced the idea of communities of value based on the need for self-actualization. To co-create meaning, customers will need to have one relationship with the organization regardless of the number of touch points with which they interact. This relationship must be one based on reciprocity rather than underpinned by roles and rules (remember Putman and Torsten). To achieve this will require a large number of connections in the organization all working towards the same aim willingly (ie releasing their discretionary effort). Not only is this logical sequence the result of the research conducted for this book, but it is also based on consistent findings that the most successful organizations tend to be the most tightly connected, where stakeholders talk to each other. They support and advise each other. They share tips and techniques. They challenge and inspire. They debate and reflect.

MAPPING YOUR 'REAL' ORGANIZATION

It has become too easy for businesses to become what some commentators have described as 'loosely coupled' organizations, where leaders are isolated from each other and functions exist on different planets. The physical, procedural and organizational structures of businesses (ie the 'formal') promote such barriers, as does the demand for staff to 'perform' alone with individual accountabilities. Formal processes and procedures for sharing knowledge about customers can only go so far. Reconnecting your business to stakeholders to ensure agility requires rich sharing and support, both of which depend on the effectiveness of the voluntary, informal, flexible and diverse interactions mapped out by the 'real'. What chance do leaders have to align 'real' agility to 'formal' objectives if they do not understand the shape of the 'real' itself? To be a connected leader requires an intimate understanding of the 'real' landscape. Connected leaders understand the networks that form the basis of the 'real' organization and their position in them. Like Kenge, leaders need a new language and perspective to map out the 'real' layer.

The actual organization is made up of connections of all shapes and sizes, amongst all stakeholders. These connections can be grouped into networks. Networks take many forms: some are productive, even critical, to the task of the organization (eg sales managers' networks across an organization or water cooler gatherings that spread communications), others are irrelevant and some are destructive. At its most basic, the 'real' is formed of groups of connections or interactions that are not hierarchical in form. Each node in the 'real' network connects to several or many other nodes.

The 'real' in practice

However, real-life 'real' organizations are complex in form. In some, connections between the nodes are very evenly distributed, whereas in others they are clumped. Some nodes are better connected than others – they are hubs. Other nodes are very poorly connected or not connected at all. Chapters 5, 6 and 7 introduced the characteristics connected leaders adopt to ensure they act as potential hubs. But what makes one node a hub and another peripheral is also a function of the topography of your 'real' organization. It doesn't matter how hard you work to become a hub for relationships if you are standing alone in a corner of the organizational galaxy. The existence of hubs and peripheries alters the flow of information and puts certain individuals in positions of considerable influence for the transmission of innovation, values and insights. It is therefore critical that, at the start of any effort you undertake to reconnect your organization to customers, you understand the make-up of the existing connections. Whilst all nodes are not equal, there are nevertheless a number of patterns that exist within 'real' organizations.

PATTERNS OF 'REAL' ORGANIZATIONS

As not everyone is equally connected, all 'real' organizations feature _hubs_ who stand head and shoulders above the rest in terms of their number of interactions with the community at large. These hubs come in two forms:

▌ _Transmitters_ initiate outgoing connections and receive fewer incoming connections (eg seek more relationships with others than others do with them).

▌ _Receivers_ on the other hand have a lot more people coming to them for advice or to form relationships but less frequently take the initiative to form such relationships.

Amongst these are a number of types that you will have within your organization. As I go through these, I am sure that names of colleagues or entire functions will come into your mind. As a starting point, it is worth noting that all 'real' organizations have hubs that can be described as power cliques.

Power cliques

Power cliques are composed of people who are well connected throughout the organization (hubs) and who interact with each other a lot. These power cliques are critical bodies within the culture of an organization. They can make or break change. The 'formal' hierarchical leadership of the organization tends to form an obvious power clique but it is not the only one.

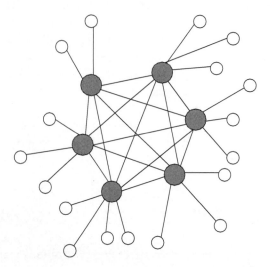

Figure 8.2   Graphical representation of a power clique

There are also mavericks (see Figure 8.3). They are influential with many people, but are not themselves connected to the elite groups. These maverick connected leaders can be destructive transmitters, whereas a maverick receiver may be operating as an agony aunt, informal counsellor or mentor to others.

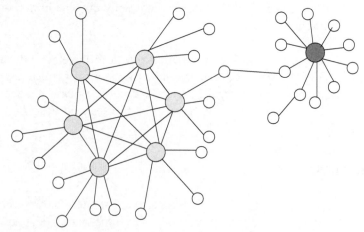

Figure 8.3   The power clique with a maverick

The problem with our Kenge-like lack of perspective lies in our tendency to see all 'formal' leadership teams as power cliques. Whilst some may be, there are also significant power cliques that reside outside the senior team. Most businesses contain at least one power clique in addition to the 'formal' leadership team. When the 'formal' leadership team is not a power clique (either composed of mavericks or of no hubs at all), the 'real' and 'formal' organizations are likely to be misaligned, leaving room for real dysfunction, which must be remedied.

Foundation networks

Beyond the power cliques lies the foundation network, or base structure of the 'real', where the bulk of rich, dense and robust connections and interactions happen.

The foundation network is composed of different numbers of emergent groups who form natural teams, where each member talks to many or all other members, but interacts far less with people outside the group (see Figure 8.4). The health of an emergent group is partly determined by the level of reciprocity among members – that is the extent to which communications flow back and forth. There are many ways in which emergent groups can be spotted. Some are organized like chains (consisting of a string of people with relationships), whilst others are small partnerships. Some people are gateways who have robust connections and act as filters of information, whilst others are interfaces (they act to facilitate liaisons between groups).

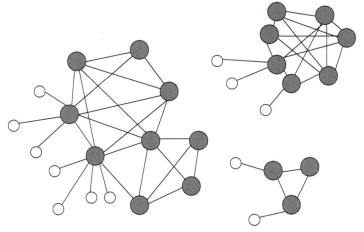

Figure 8.4 Examples of emergent groups within a foundation network

Beyond the foundation network are various isolated and neglected people. They may form partnerships outside the emergent group. They may be at the end of a long chain (see Figure 8.5). They may possess only partial connections to an emergent group. Or they may simply have very sketchy connections within the organization.

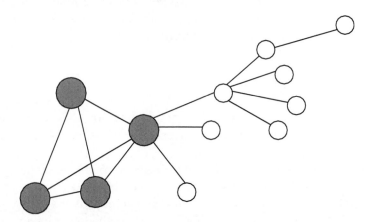

Figure 8.5   Example of a chain

These people are, in effect, wasted people economy resources. Some of them will end up connected into the main 'real' layer of the business by a single individual (often a hub in his or her own right) who brings together several such people.

CREATING A 'REAL' MAP

Before any development effort actually starts, aspiring connected leaders must bring the perspective our Kenge mindset does not understand by recognizing the power and value of their 'real' field of play. This will help leaders identify any potential obstacles or opportunities and focus their development effort. At its simplest, a connection is an interaction between two people. Often, the easiest way to understand your position in a network is simply to look at the occurrence and nature of your connections over time.

A simple exercise (which has a tendency to make me somewhat unpopular with busy executives) is to keep a record of all connections during a period of a couple of weeks. You must record not only the flow to and from but also the medium, topic and priority so as to start understanding the nature of your interactions. Having established the occurrence and the shape of the network (are you mainly connected with peers, intact team, etc?), you can then make a judgement on the nature of that connection (eg information sharing, influencing, etc). Of course, a complete enquiry requires you to be aware of what else is going on at the 'real'. You can only judge your level of connectedness if you know who else is connected and how. For example, you may be a maverick, but will only understand your position if you are aware of the connections between the power cliques. There are a number of key questions that need answering to understand fully the nature of the 'real'.

The key questions

To start identifying the nature of your 'real' organization, you can use the following questions:

▮ Can you identify any of the features described above (power cliques, mavericks, etc) in your business?

▮ Do they reinforce or conflict with the intentions expressed in your 'formal' organization?

▮ Do the emergent groups suit the flow of work and information? Do they cross over boundaries and join up the 'formal' organization?

▮ Do your senior 'formal' leaders' hubs interact effectively with one another?

▮ Who are the key opinion formers among the people in the organization at large?

▮ How extensive is the foundation network (ie the active 'real' organization)? Could it be widened to involve more people more fully in the life of the organization?

▮ Should you be looking outside to understand how other organizations or partners influence the network?

▌ Do you need more hubs in key locations to act as gateways or liaisons to unconnected groups? If so, where are they needed most?

▌ Are your hubs exercising their influence for the good of the organization or for personal agendas?

Given that their potential impact on an organization as a whole (for good or ill) is huge, power cliques deserve a special focus in any diagnostic. Their close interactions enable them to develop a shared view of the world. They speak with a single voice. These small groups reach a large proportion of the organization population. Given that their attitudes are infectious, their behaviours become common practice. Power cliques are in a position to lend weight to efforts of reform or change. They must be identified, nurtured and included to establish a culture of high expectations and to define success within the new connected organization. Without their inclusion, development efforts will be harder.

Step 2:

Map out the 'formal'/'real' gap

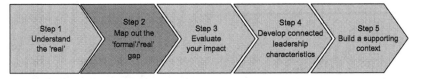

Figure 9.1   Connected leadership development, step 2

Given the strength of networks, some of the relationships formed at the 'real' can potentially become frightening sources of resistance. Whilst understanding the 'real' will ensure leaders have a complete view of the organization, it is only by measuring the gap between 'formal' and 'real' that they can put such a view in perspective (ie is the 'real'/'formal' relationship healthy or not?).

There are reasons why hubs are likely to be positive influencers. The characteristics that make an individual a hub tend to indicate that the individual is positive and enthusiastic about others and about change; otherwise, that person's impact (as defined in Chapter 3) will be limited. Acting consistently against the best interests of the organization, or in obvious conflict with senior leaders (who do still control critical levers of 'formal' power), is likely to diminish or destroy the individual's reserve of credibility.

THE GAP MATTERS

A greater risk than malicious influence or active resistance, however, is the possibility of irrelevant influence – that the connections and interactions fulfil personal and social rather than organizational goals: gossip, chatter, filling social diaries, moaning, flirting even! As James told me during our first meeting, 'I need creative people. In the nuclear industry however I don't really want a group of people wondering what would happen if they pressed a button they had been told not to press.' Yes, the 'real' is critical to success but, no, it does not contain all the answers. As mentioned in Chapter 2, to be effective an organization must be able to fulfil the complete innovation agenda. It must generate ideas, co-create products and execute. To do so requires:

▌ an *individual interface*, which is essential to *idea generation* because it provides the insights necessary for change;

▌ a set of *management processes* that ensure the *creation* of commercially viable propositions (products or services) that in turn deliver the organizational promise;

▌ a *delivery system* that is flawless in its ability to *execute* propositions time and time again.

The role of the connected leader is to ensure that the 'real' organization (the primary centre for ideas and co-creation) supports the 'formal' execution objectives. That is to say that the connected leader must ensure that:

▌ the skills and attributes of individuals are used to advance the formal agenda of the business; or/and

▌ the 'real' activities and interactions align with the tasks, demands and workflow required by the 'formal' agenda.

Remember 72.8 per cent water

Of course, it could be the 'formal' agenda that is wrong. After all, as we saw when discussing humility, connected leaders do know their limits. Whenever there is a conflict between the 'formal' structure and emergent groups it is worth at least asking whether the emergent groups have found a better way to perform tasks and are working around unhelpful organizational structures. But let's assume, for a moment, that the senior leadership of the 'formal' organization has a thoughtful and appropriate vision for the business and has taken steps to design roles, teams, reporting structures, procedures and policies that advance that vision. What then? 'Real' resistance would limit the organization's ability to deliver.

Aspiring connected leaders must understand that the opportunity offered by the 'real' is the achievement of context change resilience through organizational agility. Therefore they must be able to diagnose the gap between the 'formal' agenda and the 'real' realities. If the 'formal' objectives have been well set, the fact that the 'real' organization is potentially working against it is of worry. The solution however cannot be to coerce the 'real'. This will decrease discretionary effort and send the organization down a spiral of mediocrity. The better strategy is to understand the gap and aim to close it through active 'real' participation (ie connected leadership).

THE KEY QUESTIONS

There are some questions that help with understanding the fundamental connections between 'formal' and 'real' agendas. It is, of course, critical to remember that the 'clarity positioning system', if well applied, should ensure a profit-generating connection between 'real' and 'formal' demands. But for the sake of completeness in ensuring success in development, any aspiring connected leader should ask the following questions.

Using the network

Are you using the natural building blocks of the 'real' structure appropriately – hubs, cliques, gateways and liaisons? Do you know who they are? Are they in the right place? How would moving some of them or changing their roles affect the interconnections across the organization?

Alignment

Do the 'real' groupings match the 'formal' groupings? In particular, do all people within a function share a rich level of connections, or are some people marginalized? Are there some functions with connections that are more oriented to the outside than internally focused? Do the connections parallel the flows of work and the natural processes of the business, or are there cut-offs and barriers?

Lateral flow

By contrast, do some emergent groups cut across functional boundaries and ensure that ideas flow laterally? Are 'real' connections cutting across 'formal' functions or are they isolated? Are 'formal' functions sufficiently connected to each other at the 'real' level to ensure that they can sense and respond to changes in context that need to be addressed?

Voids

Are there any key areas without any meaningful communications? Are there barriers within the organizations at any level across which it is hard to communicate?

Transmitters versus receivers

Some people talk more than they listen: is this directly correlated with seniority or are there some senior hubs who, in addition to talking, receive incoming information?

External

Of course, it is also important that connections and conversations cross the boundaries of the organization and that people are talking to other organizations and stakeholders. Context resilience must take the outside in. Do certain people act as gateways to the whole organization, or is access more evenly distributed? How dependent are you on the gateways and are they passing on information effectively?

Closing the gap

Carrying out this enquiry will not, alone, ensure successful connected leadership development but it will at least provide leaders with an understanding of the context they operate in and how easy or hard sustaining the development effort will be.

It is critical that the answers to these questions do not lead to more 'formal' plans and organizational programmes. The value of connected leaders lies in their ability to align the 'real' to the 'formal', not 'formalize' the 'real'. Understanding the topography of the 'real' and the gaps between 'formal' and 'real' will not ensure a resilient organization. Therefore, having gained some perspective, we should now acquire a language to describe Kenge's buffaloes. Specifically, we must understand our personal starting position.

Step 3:

Evaluate your impact

Figure 10.1 Connected leadership development, step 3

The story of connected leadership is the story of impact. To be followed, an organization or a leader must be heard and seen. Without having an impact (not necessarily a loud one but at the very least a targeted one), organizations and leaders cannot make it in the people economy. This is why, having looked at the organizational dimensions that support the creation of communities, for positive development we must quickly turn to your impact. Here is a story that will help position impact in its rightful place.

iPOD LEADERSHIP

On 12 October 2005, journalists, enthusiasts and assorted stakeholders gathered at Apple's headquarters in California. To the uninitiated, the invitation was mysterious. To the millions of devoted Apple followers, however, there was no mystery. When Steve Jobs sends you a card with only the words 'one more thing' on it (the catchphrase he uses at the end of every presentation to announce the *pièce de résistance* product he is about to unleash), you know something big is afoot.

For the fans and the analysts gathered in Cupertino, California, 12 October did not disappoint. The now ubiquitous iPod acquired video capability along with a revolutionary deal with ABC to provide television content. But the 12th was also the culmination of a connected leadership journey.

The iPod is a good example of the people economy in action. Users build communities by posting reviews and opinions on the iTunes music download site. They co-create an experience by loading their favourite playlists to the site so others can purchase them. Together, the iPod, iTunes and users fulfil the co-creation and communal yearning imperatives of the people economy. However, it is not so much the iPod that is of interest here, but rather the story of Steve Jobs's leadership.

Breaking the model

The man who revolutionized and arguably saved the music industry, just as he had the film industry before (through Pixar), can teach us something fundamental about the development of connected leadership.

Too often, leaders are called to develop new skills or behaviours on the basis of a model of effectiveness. The dialogue with the HR professional goes something like this: 'We know that great leaders do A, B and C. The reason we know that is because we have studied the characteristics that differentiate our superior from our average performers. We have conducted a multi-rater survey by asking your direct reports and others for feedback on your strengths and weaknesses against these characteristics and it is clear that you need to develop B. Here are some of the recommended actions.' A logical process it may be, but it is one that is doomed to failure. There is one problem embedded in this way of thinking about the development of leadership characteristics. It does not take personal impact into account. Steve Jobs would certainly have failed in his multi-rater feedback against the connected leadership characteristics and been put on a behavioural recovery development plan by any HR department (come to think of it, most successful leaders would).

Yet Steve is a successful leader by any standard. Not only has he been capable of withstanding changes in context, but he's engineered most of them! The problem is that we apply the same logic to developing behavioural characteristics as we apply to IQ. In the same way that we believe lack of IQ means lack of ability, we believe that lack of competencies leads to lack of impact. In doing so we ignore a great part of what makes leaders successful: impact achieved through coping strategies.

Impact and characteristics

In so far as they are relationship based, coping strategies lie at the core of the 'real' layer. Their effect can only be judged by the impact of the leader. Many people lack the very competencies that, on the face of things, would lead to success, yet manage these 'deficits' through the development of powerful coping strategies. They focus on their strengths. Beethoven was deaf and yet this hardly stopped him from composing.

In this respect, Steve Jobs is the Beethoven of leadership. Driven by self-belief and entrepreneurship, he created Apple followed by NeXT. He took Pixar from being a small studio in the Lucas empire to being a key player in animated films. Given this, there would be little use anyone trying to convince Steve of a development need! To judge Steve's and any leader's effectiveness we must look at impact rather than characteristics. Indeed, it would be hard to see how a man quoted as saying 'I have a focus group every morning when I look in the mirror'[1] could be a high scorer on connected leadership characteristics. That is why 12 October was such an important date.

Linking impact and characteristics

In his presentation of 12 October, Steve used the word 'we' more than ever before. The pattern of Steve's presentations became increasingly more 'connected' from the day he announced the first iPod to the presentation on the 12th. Having lost his position at Apple, Steve could only turn into reality his dream of getting this back if he changed his impact. From the early days of his comeback at Apple to the famous presentation when he finally shed the 'interim' from his CEO title, Steve's leadership changed.

When Steve lost Apple, the impact that had made him successful in the first place had now got in the way of his success. The drive that made him so valuable to others was at the same time making it hard to generate the positive engagement he needed in the relationships that mattered. His co-workers were becoming tired of his unrealistic demands. His partners were getting increasingly tired of the high-maintenance requirements of the relationship. The focus on Jobs's needs rather than other people's desires meant that many were left disenfranchised. Altogether, Apple's executives, Disney's directors, co-workers of old and other stakeholders were becoming impatient with Jobs's disconnected attitude. From telling better-qualified engineers at Apple how to design a system to telling John Lasseter (the brain behind Pixar's success in animation) how to make films, Steve's micromanagement knew no bounds. The dreams that he so brilliantly shared to make others believe were slowly turning into nightmares. His impact was becoming so diluted that something else was needed.

Steve needed to capitalize on the goodwill generated by his comeback at Apple and engage people beyond obedience. He needed to become the moral compass of Apple to create a social commitment in the organization such as it had never had before, if it was to win again. What was he to do?

DEVELOPING STRATEGIES

All leaders develop coping strategies to compensate for their weaknesses. Some will use others to compensate for their inability to create resonance through the organization. A great CEO often cannot function without a great COO. Others will amplify their strengths so that these create more resonance than their weaknesses.

This makes impact the starting point of the development journey. Understanding your impact ensures that you concentrate development only on those characteristics that dilute your impact and for which you have no existing coping strategies. In effect, it really does not matter whether you display connected leadership behaviours as long as you have a connected leadership impact. In Steve's case, he started to recognize his team for their achievement. He let go of some of his micromanagement habits, concentrating instead on connecting people.

Maybe helped by marriage, children and a cancer from which he successfully recovered, Steve matured. Maturity of age is not the only way to achieve connected status. However, maturity of leadership is. Maturity is best described as learning to be comfortable with who we are and the impact we have. This implies understanding our behavioural limitations and how to live with them. It is this understanding of the link between our impact and our behaviours that brings value to any developmental effort.

Impact in context

For connected leaders to understand their impact, they must look at the components that form the reserve of credibility. It is this credibility that underpins the ability to influence effective hubs. The five components Chapter 3 highlighted as being at the root of credibility-based moral authority are:

- *Integrity.* The leader is honest and transparent.

- *Utility.* The leader is interested and supportive of the follower's needs.

- *Warmth.* The interaction is energizing and enjoyable.

- *Reciprocity.* Interacting with the leader is of value to both the follower and the leader (ie the follower feels that the leader not only is interested in the needs of the follower but also values his or her input to the leader's needs).

- *Maintenance.* The relationship is easy and effortless to maintain.

The starting point in developing connected leadership characteristics must be to understand your own positioning against each of these dimensions. This will enable you to define the nature of the development challenge ahead. A process of self-evaluation like the one described at the end of Part 2 can help identify the barriers to creating impact.

The result of this will lead to two courses of action: either develop the individual attributes of connected leaders (which will be the topic of step 4); or create a context within which such attributes can emerge and be used effectively (which will be the subject of step 5). The best solution is to follow both routes: individual development closely targeted to address the attributes that connect to specific weaknesses, plus generic improvement of the context.

Complex but not complicated

At the end of the diagnostic questions section of Part 3, I promised to reintroduce some element of complexity to the issue of characteristics development. So here goes. It would be too easy to assume that characteristics are simply developed by looking at the areas of impact that you are missing and developing the characteristics I have described as underpinning these areas. Each and every characteristic of connected leadership does play a role in the development of impact. Table 10.1 helps identify which characteristics relate to which area of impact. It suggests the attributes of connected leaders most closely connected with the components of credibility. It is worth noting that the list is in no way exclusive or exhaustive, merely a starting point. Because we do not rationally analyse impact as followers, we will look for a more-or-less complete package of characteristics.

Table 10.1 How the connected leadership characteristics create impact

	Integrity	Utility	Warmth	Reciprocity	Maintenance
Trust					
Trusted channel	✓	✓			
Thoughtful influence	✓		✓	✓	✓
Concern for impact	✓				✓
Meaning					
No boundaries	✓	✓		✓	
Groundwork	✓	✓	✓	✓	
Tenacity	✓	✓		✓	✓
Dialogue					
Listening first			✓	✓	✓
Humility			✓	✓	✓
Infectious passion			✓		✓

Active development

Developing the attributes themselves is less straightforward than recognizing the need for them. As with all habits, the process of change is lengthy and painful. Self-awareness is an important step, but only the first step (consider Steve Jobs's maturity). There are key principles that need to be followed for development to be successful. The route map for development is straightforward:

▌ Understand your impact, which, as highlighted in Part 2, means diagnosing your 'real' relationships with others and identifying your strengths and weaknesses.

▌ Having done so, identify the related attributes (from Table 10.1), in order to build on strengths and address weaknesses.

Step 4 turns to the development of connected leadership attributes.

Step 4:

Develop connected leadership characteristics

Figure 11.1 Connected leadership development, step 4

There are three distinct elements to the development of any leader:

▌ the behaviour and actions of the leader (the 'inputs' of leadership);

▌ the impact of the leader on other people (the 'outputs' of leadership);

▌ the culture, structure and resources within which the leader acts (the 'context' of leadership).

Having looked at your current output (ie impact), we must turn to the inputs. This will enable the creation of a focused development plan. You should not take the risk of working on your impact without understanding the behaviours and actions you are using to create it. Not only is this ineffective development, but it might also result in the unintentional destruction of what it is you do well.

In this critical step, I want to take you through the logic of behavioural development but also point out the evolution of each of the characteristics that make up the trust, meaning and dialogue model. This will enable you to keep track of where you are on the development journey.

INTEGRATED VERSUS SEQUENTIAL DEVELOPMENT

The context within which you operate will determine possible actions, which in turn determine your impact on others. Although the trust, meaning and dialogue model focuses primarily on leadership inputs, any model of leadership development that takes a single element in isolation (ie forgets about outputs or context) from others risks being irrelevant (ie the behaviours have no effect on organizational results) or unfeasible (ie they cannot be implemented in that organization). Given what we know about the importance of impact, it is critical to link all behaviours rather than think about developing them sequentially.

I have just one last bit of complexity to introduce. Throughout this book, I have highlighted the tools that connected leaders use to make their mark on the actual (eg the trust account, the positioning system). I have allocated one cluster of behaviours to each (eg the trust account is underpinned by the trust behaviours, and clarity positioning by the meaning behaviours). However, things are not that simple. Indeed, ironically perhaps, the behaviours are all connected. For example, whilst the three trust behaviours (ie trusted channel, thoughtful influence and concern for impact) ensure the trust lever is in place, as Table 11.1 shows each of the behaviours supporting the three levers of connected leadership (ie trust, meaning, and dialogue and real conversations by the dialogue behaviours) comes into play when managing a trust account.

A person's behaviour is rarely judged by any one characteristic in isolation. Combining these characteristics gives connected leaders the authenticity necessary for people to follow them. Aspiring connected leaders must therefore focus on their standing against the overall model rather than one characteristic in isolation. Also, for connected leadership,

Table 11.1 Managing a trust account

Building Trust Credit	Spending It Wisely
Trusted channel	Thoughtful influence
Listening first	No boundaries
Concern for impact	Tenacity
Infectious passion	Groundwork
Humility	

part of the context of leadership for any single individual is the leadership exercised by others. In particular, established leaders create the culture, structure and resources that help emergent hubs become more effective.

Building a connected development model

As well as the connected nature of the model, the second thing to take into account when planning for the development of connected leadership behaviours is the nature of the interactions between people and context.

So far, in considering connected leadership, the trust, meaning and dialogue model has focused primarily on inputs by describing a model of the behaviours observed as common to connected leaders. We have also touched upon outputs by exploring the relevance of these behaviours. In so far as the model presents the positive relationship between connected leaders and their environment, we have also begun to examine context. However, there are many other ways in which context is important.

There are, therefore, two steps to developing a more connected style of leadership, either in yourself or in others:

1. Evaluate your impact on others, through their perceptions of the credibility and trust you have established with each of them.

2. Work backwards from these findings to select and develop the characteristics that could make a difference. This is why step 3 is a critical step in ensuring the development actions focus on the right characteristics.

Levels of development

Amplifying strengths or addressing weaknesses requires an understanding of where these come from. As we have seen so far, any leadership success or failure is always a function of perception. The same is true of development successes.

Figure 11.2   Underpinnings of a development plan

In fact, there are three crucial perceptions that have to be aligned for change, as shown in Figure 11.2. We need to believe:

▌ that it is the right thing to do;

▌ that it is within our potential; and

▌ that it is part of the role we fulfil.

The latter is often the chief barrier to development, especially among middle managers who instead see the maintenance of the 'formal' delivery mechanisms as their chief responsibility.

As observed in Chapter 4, our role models and images of leaders are too often rooted in the 'formal' organization model. The Kenge story used at the beginning of Part 4 explains why. In essence, we all have differing perspectives of leadership informed by our experiences of 'growing up' as leaders. We therefore need to spend some time debating and reflecting upon our perceptions of leadership, as a foundation to changing our habits.

Developing awareness

Once values, role models and self-image are aligned, the best recipe for behavioural development is a rolling combination of reflection and practice. Theory without action is irrelevant; action without theory is instinct and therefore hard to replicate and share (remember that the value of connected leaders comes from their ability to make others grow). To generate a change in practice that can be sustained in a flexible way within a variety of new situations, we need a combination of both.

Development at the 'real' level is best achieved in collaboration with others. Experienced leaders use the connected leadership ideas as tools, to be criticized, amended and adapted (ie the topic of sustained dialogue), rather than a mantra to be obeyed. The development journey itself forms part of creating new 'real' reflexes and habits.

The key questions

A collective reflection on the development of connected leadership can start with the following diagnostic questions:

▌ Does the 'investing and spending wisely' model reflect our experience? Are there other analogies that mean more to us?

▌ Are there other tactics or behaviours that might also fit the bill?

▌ Are there times when it is appropriate to spend unwisely or to take a gamble?

▌ Do we need more connected leaders or a combination of traditional and connected leaders?

▌ What does 'listening first', for example, look like in practice? What are the pitfalls? What are unusual or hidden ways of achieving it?

▌ What feels natural or authentic or honest to us?

▌ Why do colleagues choose not to be connected? What are the incentives in the system?

▌ What are the limits and limitations of this approach?

DEVELOPING CHARACTERISTICS

There are many actions that can be taken to develop each of the connected leadership behaviours. Along with the description of the behaviours, in the chapters on trust, meaning and dialogue, came indications of possible development actions (remembering again that early actions are an important facet of connected leadership development). Indeed, each chapter also gave indications of actions and behaviours that get in the way of the characteristics.

Given the number of levels at which development investment needs to be targeted, the following sections give some indications of how each characteristic looks for emerging leaders and established connected leaders. Questions are included that not only help refine the area for development but also highlight the increase in breadth of each behaviour as the leader's development journey progresses. The idea is that for each, given the levels at which you operate (as analysed by the diagnostic questions at the end of Part 3), you can use one of the tables below (Tables 11.2 to 11.10) to understand what the next stage of your development looks like for each of the characteristics.

DEVELOPING TRUST

Trusted channel

The progression from emerging to established connected leader is best described as moving from giving direct advice and guidance to setting the scene.

▌ How often do people turn to you for advice? What do you know that others might need?

Table 11.2   Emerging and established manifestations of trusted channel

Emerging Connected Leaders	Established Connected Leaders
Helpful	Providing information that encourages reflection
Offering advice to others	Opening others' horizons
Hands on	Big picture
Providing training to others	Changing others' expectations

Thoughtful influence

Progressing from emerging to established connected leader is about changing one's sphere of influence from the concrete and interpersonal to the abstract and organizational. This characteristic is more common at established than emerging levels.

▌ How well thought through are your attempts to influence? Are you aware of and responsive to the reactions of your audience?

Table 11.3   Emerging and established manifestations of thoughtful influence

Emerging Connected Leaders	Established Connected Leaders
Target those in influence	Sell ideas to all
Interpersonal level	System level
Small scale (few people at once)	Large groups

Concern for impact

Developing concern for impact is about enlarging the extent of your concern from individuals to the bigger picture.

▌ What makes you tick? What would you like to be known for? What will be your legacy?

Table 11.4   Emerging and established manifestations of concern for impact

Emerging Connected Leaders	Established Connected Leaders
Think about impact upon others, judging and evaluating past interventions	Wider and longer view of reputation
Wrestle with conflict between involvement and intrusion	Worry less about ups and downs of individual relationships
Think about others' perceptions of them	More secure in their reputation

DEVELOPING MEANING

No boundaries

Developing no boundaries is about changing the focus from 'intact' to 'impact' team.

▌ How often do you get involved or make an input outside your comfort zone?

Table 11.5 Emerging and established manifestations of no boundaries

Emerging Connected Leaders	Established Connected Leaders
Refer to policies and procedures to justify interventions	Refer to vision and meaning to justify interventions
Think about themselves as 'one of the team'	Think about themselves as conveners of teams
Tentative in intervening	Forceful in intervening
Emotive in intervening	Objective in intervening

Groundwork

Groundwork development is best described as working on the ability to move from being reactive to being proactive.

▌ How much task work do you actually do?

Table 11.6 Emerging and established manifestations of groundwork

Emerging Connected Leaders	Established Connected Leaders
Personally well organized	Concern with processes and procedures
Follow up on commitments and promises	Embed commitment and follow-through into the organization itself

Tenacity

Developing tenacity is about moving from being tenacious to being flexible.

Table 11.7 Emerging and established manifestations of tenacity

Emerging Connected Leaders	Established Connected Leaders
Tenacious	Flexible
Use reputation to develop connections	Work through others to develop connections
Reliable	Set agendas
See things through	Adapt to events as they unfold

▌ How stubborn are you about your ends and how flexible are your means?

DEVELOPING DIALOGUE

Listening first

Table 11.8   Emerging and established manifestations of listening first

Emerging Connected Leaders	Established Connected Leaders
Interpersonal	Systemic
Good listener	Planned and systematic listening
Enable others to take active role in conversations	Create systems, structure and culture for debate and input
Reactive	Proactive creation of listening organization

Developing listening first means increasing one's impact from good listening to creating open organizations.

▌ How many ideas and strategies do you receive, digest and use from other people?

Humility

Table 11.9   Emerging and established manifestations of humility

Emerging Connected Leaders	Established Connected Leaders
Acknowledge and learn from mistakes	Know limits in advance
Seek help to repair errors	Seek help before trouble
Get timely support	Create enduring support networks

Developing humility means learning to be proactive in the way that you apply it.

▌ Do you know your own boundaries and limits? Do you actively work with others to surmount these?

Infectious passion

Table 11.10 Emerging and established manifestations of infectious passion

Emerging Connected Leaders	Established Connected Leaders
Exhibit enjoyment of role and situation Positive about existing organization	Positive towards change Express excitement and optimism about new ways of doing things

Having an infectious passion means being able to move from defending the status quo to embracing change.

▌ Do you make people feel better about the situation? Would anyone choose to work with you?

DEVELOPMENT TACTICS

In the same way as aspiring connected leaders need to understand their impact, they need to find their voice when it comes to exhibiting these characteristics. I often recall the story of the leader who asked me to gather feedback from his direct reports on how effective he had been at using a more authoritative style of leadership. When I told one of his direct reports about the leader's intent, his thoughtful reply was 'I see. So that's what you call authoritative. We've just been calling it weird!' Trying to be what you are not is not the recipe to successful development of a more authentic style. There are some tactics that one can apply to develop a more connected mindset.

TWISTED development

Adaptability has always been an important competency for any leader. But to be successful in the development of connected leadership characteristics, leaders need to embrace a new way of thinking that moves beyond flexibility. When looking into some of the paradoxes of connected leadership and talking to passionate connected leaders, I have come to call connected leaders 'twisted' rather than flexible. This has come to provide me with a good mnemonic to remember the tactics for change:

▌ Think differently. Identify and explain to others the filters that make you see facts in a certain way. Facts are only facts depending on how you look at them. Sharing your filters ensures others can table their views.

▌ Walk in other people's shoes. Always ask yourself what it must feel like to be in someone else's shoes. Empathy is a precondition of connected impact.

▌ In sync. Align what you think with what you say and what you say with what you do. The authenticity this creates will give you other people's support.

▌ Share everything. Make sure you talk about your own desires, feelings and actions rather than just the organizational need.

▌ Turn your tongue. My mother used to tell me to turn my tongue in my mouth seven times before speaking, which would give me enough time to think about what I was about to say. Make sure you have this kind of self-control so as to judge your impact.

▌ Explain well. Make sure that people know what your standards are, and seek feedback to ensure your messages are understood.

▌ Dream vividly. Tell stories that engage and inspire rather than just tell others what to do.

Your behaviours and your tactics will help you develop. Creating a context to support your development effort will ensure sustainability.

Step 5:

Build a supporting context

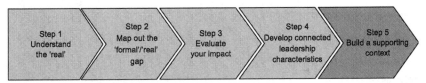

Figure 12.1 Connected leadership development, step 5

Given our 'formal' heritage, we all have a tendency to think about development in linear terms. We worry about whether the leader or the context needs to be developed first. The reality, as we have seen, of any development is that each element impacts the other. The 'real' layer is a dynamic system of relationships and, because of this, both the leader and the context must develop in parallel. In addition, context development will sustain our need to connect the new world with the old (which has demonstrated its value albeit without context resilience), thus sustaining motivation.

Right from the Introduction, I mentioned that the failure of many development strategies in organizations is the sole focus on the leader.

Leaders cannot develop in isolation from the context. Recently I was asked by a CEO to facilitate the development of a new type of leadership that would help break down the silo mentality of leaders in the organization. It became clear, however, quite quickly that leadership was not the main issue. I know many of you will have had negative experiences with consultants trying to change the brief but I can assure you that in this case the problem was not rephrased by me for the purpose of expending a revenue stream! Quite simply, in the case of this organization, the roles themselves were designed for the purpose of sole accountability. Little in the role was constructed for collaboration. Basically, even if they wanted to, leaders had no chance ever to cross boundaries imposed by their roles.

CONTEXTUAL IMPROVEMENT

If steps 1 and 2 were about getting a picture of the field of development and steps 3 and 4 were about understanding your impact and changing it through development, then step 5 on our development journey must be about making development efforts sustainable by going beyond the individual. Apart from leaders' own behaviour and effectiveness, there are a number of elements of context that will help leaders become more connected and stay that way.

Opportunity

Whatever the skills, people won't connect unless they can come together. What opportunities do people have to work together in groups, either face to face or virtually? How well do such groups work? How are the roles constructed? Is there any scope for individuals to go beyond their set of accountabilities and be encouraged to do so? How hard is it for people to go beyond the boundaries of their roles?

Clarity

People can negotiate the utility and reciprocity in their relationships much more effectively when you have helped to clarify their individual goals (role) and the wider organizational mission (strategy, priorities, vision). While freedom to act helps relationships, ambiguity of purpose hinders them. How often do individuals participate in the 'formal' direction-setting efforts of the business? Do people understand the difference between accountabilities and priorities? Are interdependencies surfaced and managed?

Mediation

Established connected leaders can create the context for, and support, emerging connected leaders. Do you know who the established connected leaders are? Do you know who your emerging connected leaders are? Are they isolated or supported in their efforts? How much latitude can be afforded at the 'formal' to facilitate their development efforts?

Culture

The norms of the organization, what is valued, what is believed, what is acceptable and what is noticed can help or hinder interconnections. In particular, most organization cultures specify a certain 'etiquette' for communication that may be more or less effective. Such norms are built from the role models, rituals and ceremonies of organizational life. Are you aware of the culture of your business? Which artefacts need to change? What are the balance and the tone of conversations in the organization? Are any stories being told about the value of the 'real', or are only 'formal' achievements rewarded? Remember that all 'formal' achievements, if they are sustainable, have roots in the 'real'.

Balance

To bring warmth, humour and above all infectious passion to relationships, people need space to breathe, opportunities to play, freedom from pressure and stress and a sense of perspective. These are rare in today's organizations. The challenge for any leader is to understand how much of the pressure is real and how much is the result of a 'formal' need for activity (regardless of output). Over the last few years I have seen the emergence of a certain directive style of leadership in organizations. I am always told that the world of business is becoming so tough that only such a directive style can be effective. Clearly, the message in this book is that it is only effective in getting individuals to do what you want them to do. However, it will not be effective in getting your customers to follow, as you will be actively destroying the social networks that foster communities of value. In people economy organizations, balance is everything.

Freedom

Relationships form most effectively when they are voluntary. How much opportunity do people have to determine their own working practices and choose their relationships? Again, what constraints do roles place on individuals? What, in the way leadership is used in the organization, helps and hinders the formation of connections? Ultimately, we all have choices, but some choices can be so hard to make that it is easy to see how the context might be restricting individuals' freedom.

IMPACT AS THE KEY TO UNLOCKING CONNECTIONS

Aspiring connected leaders must understand that their strength comes from their impact. The aim is therefore to have a connected impact rather than connected leadership characteristics per se. This means two things: 1) developing coping strategies to remedy a lack of impact is as important as developing connected characteristics; and 2) developing characteristics can only be effective if leaders are going to be authentic by finding their own connected voice rather than following someone else's model (otherwise the impact will be lessened).

The connected journey summary

Leaders who want their connected leadership development efforts to be sustainable will need to look at their impact and understand the characteristics that need development. They will then need to understand at what level development efforts need to be targeted. The three key levels of development that need to be addressed to target efforts at the right level are:

▌ *Values.* 'I believe it is the right thing to do.'

▌ *Self-image.* 'It is within my potential.'

▌ *Social role.* 'It is part of the role that I fulfil.'

Each characteristic can then be developed by taking into account the stage of leadership maturity at which the leader operates. Emerging leaders often need to broaden their impact as well as change the image they have of their role in order to be successful.

Connected leaders understand that flexibility is a necessary but not differentiating characteristic of leadership. As well as being flexible they have to create a context that will support their developmental needs. To do so they concentrate on the main levers of a connected organization:

▌ *Opportunity.* Are there enough opportunities to connect?

▌ *Clarity.* Do we have the clarity of goal and mission that will show us the need to connect?

▌ *Mediation.* Do established leaders create the support for connections?

▌ *Culture.* Do we value and encourage connections?

▌ *Balance.* Do we have a balance in the messages that we communicate or are they primarily 'formal'?

▌ *Freedom.* Are people free to choose their relationships?

It is that balance between understanding personal development needs and tackling contextual hygiene factors that gives real traction to connected leadership development efforts. Connected leadership is the story of leaders *and* organizations. Communities inside and outside the organization need to be fostered and, for this to happen, leaders must make sure that they develop the type of organization that will best bring these communities about. There is a lot resting on the shoulders of today's leaders but, at the risk of losing the patient readership that has made it to the end of the book, I do maintain that not as much as we think is down to one person or a top team alone. Organizations are complex human systems that are shaped by the many variables of the context they operate in. As leaders you have a disproportionate influence on the context, but you are not the sole influence. This leads me to some concluding thoughts.

THE LEADERSHIP TAKEAWAY

Here are the points from Part 4 that are pertinent to the way you think about leadership. No one would dream of running a marathon without first getting into shape, or at least no one would ever assume he or she could be successful without first being healthy. 'Getting into shape' for aspiring connected leaders means understanding both the nature of the 'real' organization and their impact within it.

Step 1: Understand the 'real'.

- First, aspiring connected leaders must understand that the 'real' organization does not follow 'formal' rules. However, it can be mapped out and deconstructed to provide a route map for navigation.
- This is important, as it will help leaders understand the context for development.

Step 2: Map out the 'formal'/'real' gap.

- Leaders must then understand the nature of the connection between the 'formal' objectives and the 'real' organization. This will provide leaders with an understanding of the challenges and opportunities ahead.

Step 3: Evaluate your impact.

- To diagnose their impact, connected leaders should examine how credible they are in the eyes of others. That credibility, and therefore connected leaders' potential effectiveness, comes from each relationship being judged by followers against five criteria: integrity, utility, warmth, reciprocity and maintenance.
- When it comes to developing connected leadership characteristics, you must act with passion. Actions create a virtuous development cycle. Whether you succeed or fail you are creating impact, which, as long as you are open enough about your intent, will give others the opportunity to engage with you. This will enable you to develop not just yourself but the context around you (which in turn will support your development).

Step 4: Develop connected leadership characteristics.

– Having understood your impact, you must think about the coping strategies you can apply to mitigate your weaknesses whilst you emphasize your strengths. Only then can you focus on the behaviours that you need to develop. In order to do so you need to understand whether you must develop new skills or find new ways of looking at your role.

– To ensure that the development effort does not lead you to act in inauthentic ways, you must ensure that you build on what you are already doing rather than completely rethink your approach.

Step 5: Build a supporting context.

– The context often dictates the opportunities you have for development. By ensuring that the organization is receptive to its 'real' layer (ie by creating opportunities to engage in relationships), you will sustain your development effort.

– Do not forget to be yourself.

Concluding thoughts

If you want the rainbow, you've got to put up with the rain.
Dolly Parton

There is a long way to go before we understand the full implications of the people economy. Connected leadership itself, as a dynamic, network-based form of leadership, is only in its infancy. Yet, regardless of future developments, the fact that its roots lie in relationships takes us back to a time when businesses derived value (financial viability and sustainability) from their deep relationships with people.

To yearn for times past is a futile game. The old days are not always the best. Positive advances in knowledge in every field of human endeavour have been phenomenal. Charlotte, my eight-year-old daughter, has never seen a phone with a wire, and George, her four-year-old brother, sees wi-fi as nothing other than ordinary. My sister and I used to rejoice in our great-grandmother's stories of a world without cars. We thought she must have been born in the Middle Ages! In the last four generations, planes have taken to the sky. We have been on the moon. We have dived deeper in the oceans than ever before. We have seen inside our bodies, first in black and white and then in colour. We have even mapped the very essence of human life.

Yet to see change as inherently beneficial is also misguided. Access to these developments has been slower for some than for others. If your home has something other than a dirt floor, you are in the top half of the world's population. If your home has a roof, a door, windows and more than one room, you are in the top 20 per cent. If you have refrigeration in your home, you are in the top 5 per cent. If you have a car, a video or DVD player, a computer and a microwave, then you are in the top 1 per cent.[1]

Without any moral judgement about whether this is a better or worse world than the one handed on to us by our parents, we must learn from history and live in the present. The sum total of reserves of trust and credibility between members of an organization is a measure of social capital. We know that social capital built on connections between people and businesses has created greater value in the past than we have been able to capture for some time.

We have striven to re-create these relationships by endeavouring to engineer businesses on a human scale using the technological tools now at our disposal. But our efforts at creating a one-to-one marketing world, whilst well intended (in so far as they were created to increase the personalization of an experience), are doomed to failure. Tools certainly make the lack of relationship more bearable but they do not fill the void in meaning that human beings are experiencing.

Despite the complexity built into today's organizations, relationships have not become more complex. They might have become more complicated to sustain, using our 'formal' tools, but the richness of connections experienced at the 'real' layer of the organization shows that they are still simple (at least for human *beings*) to foster.

For business to have any sustainable future in the face of change and for organizations to develop the agility necessary for context resilience, leaders need to reconnect with the 'real' organization. It is a sad truth and a sad indictment of our work as leaders that our future success rests on our ability to relearn how to socialize. This book is an attempt at starting a conversation that, it is hoped, will lead to the co-creation of a new meaning for leadership.

Dolly Parton is right: the rainbow does require rain, but, as any child knows (and we were all children once upon a time), the rainbow has magical properties that make the journey fulfilling despite the rain. Business leaders who have forgotten the magic of childhood should remember that there is also a pot of gold at the end of the rainbow. I hope that this fact alone sustains you on your journey to developing as a connected leader.

Notes

INTRODUCTION

1. Margaret Thatcher (1996) *The Path to Power*, HarperCollins, London.

PART 1

1. Mori (2003).
2. Worldwatch Institute (2004) State of the World.
3. Simon Zadek (2001) *Third Generation Corporate Citizenship: Public policy and business in society*, Foreign Policy Centre, London.
4. On 12 November 2004, the Federal Trade Commission ruled that telemarketers could in fact use pre-recorded messages to contact individuals who had registered on the 'do not call' list, presumably on the basis that it is easier for people to put the phone down on a computer.

CHAPTER 1

1. Mihaly Csikszentmihalyi (2002) *Flow: The classic work on how to achieve happiness*, Rider & Co, London.
2. Abraham Maslow (1970) *Motivation and Personality*, 2nd edn, Harper & Row, New York.
3. John Grant (2000) *The New Marketing Manifesto: The 12 rules for building successful brands in the 21st century*, Texere Publishing, New York.
4. National Association of Anorexia Nervosa and Associated Disorders, www.anad.org/site/anadweb/content.php?type=1&id=6982.
5. George W Abbott, Jr and Lee S Sporn (2001) *Trademark Counterfeiting*, S. Rep. No. 104-177, 104th Cong., 1st Sess. 1-2 (1995).
6. Stephen Dowling (2004) Taking opera to the cheap seats, *BBC News Online*, 15 April.
7. Viktor E Frankl (1986) *Man's Search for Meaning*, Simon & Schuster, New York.
8. Robert Putman (2000) *Bowling Alone: The collapse and revival of American community*, Simon & Schuster, New York.
9. Ronald Inglehart (1990) *Culture Shift in Advanced Industrial Society*, Princeton University Press, Princeton, NJ.
10. *Yearbook of International Organisations*, Union of International Organisations, Brussels.
11. For more information see www.MariaSchneider.com.

CHAPTER 2

1. For more on the rules of golf I would strongly recommend Jeffrey S Kuhn and Bryan A Garner (2004) *The Rules of Golf in Plain English*, University of Chicago Press, Chicago, IL.
2. Frederick P Brooks (1995) *The Mythical Man-Month*, Addison Wesley, Boston, MA.
3. These extracts from *Made in America* by Sam Walton can be found on Wal-Mart's corporate website at www.Walmart.com.
4. Charles Fishman (2003) The Wal-Mart you don't know, *Fast Company*, 77, December.
5. A Bianco and W Zellner (2003) Is Wal-Mart too powerful?, *Business Week*, 6 October.
6. *Independent*, London, 2 June 2005.

CHAPTER 3

1. Whirlpool finds its cool, _Fast Company_, June 2005.
2. There are a number of studies which have looked at and calculated the impact of the release of discretionary effort on organizational performance. In particular the following documents have looked at the impact and set out the dimensions which have been replicated in numerous sectors and countries. LOMA (Lynn G Merritt) and the Hay Group (Martin Leshner, PhD, David A Baker, John B Larrere, Stephen P Kelner, Jr, PhD, and Daniel Williams), 1994, _Leadership for the 21st Century: Life Insurance Leadership Study_. Becklean, W & M Kinkead (1968), _The Organizational Audit: A Management Assessment Technique_, Boston Harvard Business School. _Report to Baron, Inc., on the Effects of Workshops on Managing Motivation after Six Months_ (1973), Boston McBer and Company, Inc. _Confidential Report to Fortune 100 Company_ (1979), Boston McBer and Company, Inc. Hay Group.
3. Connected leadership: a model of influence for those without power, Hay Group, April 2005.

CHAPTER 5

1. Spider in banana bunch bites man, bbc.co.uk, BBC News, 18 June 2004.
2. Spider invasion sends mum bananas, bbc.co.uk, BBC News, 22 June 2004.
3. M Lefkowitz, RR Blake and JS Mouton (1955) Status factors in pedestrian violation of traffic signals, _Journal of Abnormal and Social Psychology_, 51, pp 704–06.
4. For some examples of how we make decisions, you can turn to Malcolm Gladwell (2005) _Blink: The power of thinking without thinking_, Allen Lane, London.
5. Hay Group research conducted on 'Working with emotional intelligence' by Daniel Goleman.
6. Henley Centre (1999) Planning for consumer change report.

CHAPTER 7

1. There are a lot of references to Anokhin's claims in creativity literature. His main published work where his theory is expanded is PK Anokhin (1968) _Biology and Neurophysiology of the Conditioned Reflex_, Medicina, Moscow.

2. Anokhin (1968).
3. T Armstrong (1987) *In Their Own Way: Discovering and encouraging your child's personal learning style*, Jeremy P Tarcher, Los Angeles.
4. US Patent Activity Calendar Years 1790–2001, with data extracted from the US Patent Statistics Report, March 2002, US Patent and Trademark Office (USPTO), and from the USPTO TAF database. Many of the older statistics are obtained from the Technology Assessment and Forecast Seventh Report, March 1977, USPTO.

PART 4

1. CM Turnbull (1961) Some observations regarding the experiences and behavior of the BaMbuti Pygmies, *American Journal of Psychology*, 74, pp 304–08. Copyright 1961 by the Board of Trustees of the University of Illinois.

STEP 3

1. There are a large number of stories emanating from a large number of books written about Steve Jobs. For an in-depth, well-documented account of Steve Jobs's leadership and the changes that have occurred as his leadership matured, I recommend Jeffrey S Young and William L Simon (2005) *iCon: Steve Jobs – the greatest second act in the history of business*, John Wiley, Hoboken, NJ.

CONCLUDING THOUGHTS

1. Caux Round Table (CRT), an international network of business leaders working to promote a moral capitalism.

Index

With over 42 years of publishing, more than 80 million people have succeeded in business with thanks to **Kogan Page**

www.koganpage.com